Evangelical Does Not Equal Republican . . . or Democrat

Also by Lisa Sharon Harper

An' Push da Wind Down:
A Play in Two Acts

Evangelical Does Not Equal Republican . . . or Democrat

Lisa Sharon Harper

THE NEW PRESS

NEW YORK
LONDON

Unless otherwise indicated, Scripture quotations
are from the New Revised Standard Version of the Bible,
copyright © 1989 by the Division of Christian Education of the National
Council of Churches of Christ in the United States of America.

Published in the United States by The New Press, New York, 2008
Distributed by W. W. Norton & Company, Inc., New York

LIBRARY OF CONGRESS CATALOGING-IN-PUBLICATION DATA

Harper, Lisa, 1963–
Evangelical does not equal Republican . . . or Democrat /
Lisa Sharon Harper.
    p.   cm.
Includes bibliographical references.
ISBN 978-1-59558-419-9 (hc.)
1. Evangelicalism—United States.   2. Christianity and politics—
United States.   I. Title.
BR516.H254   2008
277.3'083—dc22   2008016239

The New Press was established in 1990 as a not-for-profit alternative to
the large, commercial publishing houses currently dominating the book
publishing industry. The New Press operates in the public interest rather
than for private gain, and is committed to publishing, in innovative ways,
works of educational, cultural, and community value that are often deemed
insufficiently profitable.

www.thenewpress.com

Composition by dix!
This book was set in New Caledonia

Printed in the United States of America

2   4   6   8   10   9   7   5   3   1

To my mother,
Sharon Lawrence Harper,
who lulled me to sleep singing "Wade in the Water"
and planted dreams of Freedom Land in my soul

O, Freedom!
O, Freedom!
O, freedom over me.
An' before I be a slave
I be buried in my grave
And go home to my Lord
And be free.

—Traditional African American spiritual

Contents

Foreword

Evangelical Does Not Equal Republican . . . or Democrat is a gift to us all.

I've read many books on justice and reconciliation over the years. We've had some good ones. Most focus on reconciliation stories. Some focus on theology; others on history. Lisa Sharon Harper combines historical analysis, theological savvy, and sociological insight, and she puts things in order while telling a great story. Lisa speaks with a strong and unique evangelical voice. Her perspectives—growing up a black evangelical and a woman—add a critical yet personal edge to our analysis of the evangelical church. She clarifies where we've come from, how we've wandered so far from "our roots"—as she puts it—and how we are finding our way back to the holistic good news.

The Bible says humans were created in the image of God. The United States Declaration of Independence says, "We hold these truths to be self-evident, that all men are created equal." That eternal truth is so profound: that all humans "are endowed by their Creator with certain inalienable rights, that among these are life, liberty, and the pursuit of happiness." But those in power mocked that self-evident truth. They turned around and created a slavocracy, justified through their religion. Even though times changed and manifestations of racism changed, the church was still at the center of the racism equation in America. Racism is hypocrisy, the way we practice it in America—the way we have practiced it in the church. We smile with our faces but curse our neighbors in our hearts, in our relations, through our structures, and through our politics.

In 1947, Carl F.H. Henry, a theological giant in the evangelical world, wrote *The Uneasy Conscience of Modern Fundamentalism.* This postwar book urged evangelicals (called "fundamentalists" at the time) to address the social ills of the world around them. Fundamentalists were known for their political isolationism. He said if they carried the good news of Jesus to the world, they would find that good news relevant to the ills of society. But there was a problem and evangelicals knew it. Their message was not holistic. They recognized that the message they had was not relevant to the plight of people pressed to the margins of the world. Hence, in response to Henry's call, evangelicals deliberately said, "You blacks reach blacks." And they released themselves from the responsibility to fix their own truncated and, therefore, impotent *news.*

I like the idea that we are stewards of God's good news. I have spent my life trying to steward a holistic understanding of that good news to my generation. Tom Skinner, Jim Wallis, Tony Campolo, Ron Sider, and I came from the same generation, and we've been at this work a long time. Maybe we could have done better. We did what we could. Lisa Sharon Harper represents a new generation of evangelicals wrestling to understand the gospel for their generation. By the very fact that they are more diverse in race and gender than my generation and are more global in outlook, they are already moving the good news forward. I am hopeful. I feel a sense of gratitude now. A new generation of young people is struggling to discover the holistic truth of the gospel. This is exciting!

Lisa Sharon Harper's voice emerges from this struggle to offer clarity in the midst of confusing times. To my knowledge, evangelicals in the United States have never had such outstanding theological work come from a black evangelical woman. As a result, *Evangelical Does Not Equal Republican . . . or Democrat* holds great potential to connect the prophets of my era to emerging evangelical leaders. Lisa understands her evangelical roots and the importance of honoring and learning from them. In addition, this book builds a bridge to the secular society and the media, which has misunderstood our evangelical heritage for long enough. Lisa's analysis offers historical, sociological, and theological perspectives that shed light on things for all of us.

Today's world is plagued by political confusion and partisan division. This book is a call for unification beyond political lines. Lisa looks beyond Republicans or Democrats as the agents of a just solution. People always ask me, "What would this just solution look like?" Well, we don't quite know what it's going to look like. What we do know is that it starts with biblical truth.

I strongly recommend this book for any and all who want that truth to have its impact.

John M. Perkins
Founder of the John M. Perkins Foundation for
Reconciliation and Development and co-founder of
the Christian Community Development Association
Jackson, Mississippi

Evangelical Does Not Equal
Republican . . . or Democrat

Introduction

A seismic shift is rumbling underfoot in evangelical America. Its impact promises to affect not only politics in the United States, but the world. This is not a shift from the Right to the Left. It is not a shift from one set of values to another. Nor is it from one political party to another. This shake-up has been a long time coming. Some of us can feel the shock waves already. We feel its early impact in public life and sense that something is changing, but what? How? Why?

This book tells the story of a quake with broad social implications. It is shaking the heart of evangelical America and is transforming evangelical belief and action. Evangelical perceptions of the gospel, literally "good news," itself are morphing. Cracks are opening that expose something old—very old—under the ground of today's evangelicals. A growing number of evangelicals are rediscovering the good news that belonged to their forebearers in the late eighteenth and early nineteenth centuries. That good news led evangelicals to work for the poor, the marginalized, and the oppressed by campaigning to end slavery, laying foundations for women's suffrage, and forming labor unions.[1]

Today, that rediscovered good news is compelling a new generation of evangelicals to lead and support multiple national and international reform movements. Evangelicals are signing antipoverty, antitorture, and environmental stewardship declarations. They are fighting for workers' rights as well as immigration reform; and they are leading the global movement to stop sex slavery. The good news that rocked three continents in the eighteenth and nineteenth centuries is, once again, making a broad social and political impact within U.S. public life. Evangelicals are reembracing the gospel, however, with a new, postmodern twist.

This postmodern evangelical era is moving away from polarized dichotomies. The sharply divided fights of the past, such as the liberal social gospel versus the fundamentalist personal gospel, seem irrelevant. An inclusive approach to biblical interpretation motivates twenty-first-century evangelicals. They reevaluate twentieth-century polemics through this inclusive approach because of their commitment to a Christ-centered worldview and the Protestant Reformation's principle of *sola scriptura*, giving primary authority to the biblical text. With this postmodern commitment, evangelicals are reembracing the good news of social transformation, even as they retain their commitment to personal transformation.

As twenty-first-century evangelicals reconnect with Jesus's teachings on poverty and oppression, they are emphasizing how he aligned himself with the poor and oppressed. Thus, this new generation is finding itself in alignment with the marginalized of society. It is this new alignment that is beginning to rock the politics and work of evangelicals. What pundits have categorized as a political shift is actually profoundly theological and spiritual. It is the product of a broadening evangelical worldview spurred by new readings of the gospel.

UNUSUAL POLITICS

Much has been said about evangelical voters since the midterm elections of 2006. In the days leading up to the election, many pundits thought evangelicals would carry the swing states. It turned out they did not. A 2006 midterm election exit poll revealed evangelicals voted largely the same as they did in the 2004 congressional races. Seventy-two percent voted for Republican congressional candidates in this election compared to 75 percent in 2004, and the 78 percent of white evangelical Republican support for George W. Bush in 2004 dropped slightly, by 6 percent, in 2006. However, when white evangelicals were asked if they approved of 2006 Democratic policies and plans for the future, they were nearly evenly split; 32 percent said they approved, while 37 percent said they disapproved. It is striking that *only* 37 percent disapproved. Another 31 percent of evangelical voters remained undecided. They were not sure if they approved or disapproved of Democratic Party policies. If we remove the 27 percent of white evangelicals who voted Democratic from the equation, 36 percent of white evangelicals voting Republican did not necessarily disapprove of the Democratic Party. This begs the question: why did they vote Republican?[2]

There was another kicker in 2006. While 72 percent of white evangelicals voted for Republican candidates, 41 percent of them said they were *happy the Democrats won* the midterm election. Go figure. Another 41 percent said they were unhappy and 18 percent said they did not know how they felt. Thus, when the 27 percent of white evangelicals who voted Democratic are removed from the count, at least 41 percent of white evangelicals who voted Republican were happy the Democrats won! And another 18 percent voted

Republican with weak support for their own choice. This kind of wavering Republican support among white evangelicals seemed implausible in 2004 when strong white evangelical support made up the largest single Republican voting bloc, fully 35 percent, of Bush's presidential electoral support. Compare that to the single largest Democratic voting bloc, African Americans, which came in at 21 percent of Democratic support in 2004.[3]

Can the exit polls be trusted? They seem to indicate that evangelical loyalty to the Republican Party may be unraveling. I suggest they are a sign of the shake-up rocking the evangelical world. When I was approached to write this book, I had a sense that this shake-up was underway, but I had no hard evidence outside of the exit polls and my own experience. Now, I also have evidence from sixty-seven interviews with prominent Christian leaders, most of them evangelical. Virtually everyone I asked agreed to be interviewed for this book—perhaps because I, too, am an evangelical.

TWIN CONVERSIONS

I was born again on August 21, 1983, at a rural, white, evangelical Sunday evening church camp meeting, outside Cape May, New Jersey. My spiritual rebirth in high school was quickly followed by a political conversion. Within months, Ronald Reagan ran for his second presidential term against former vice president Walter Mondale.

With my new born-again fervor, I scared my eight-year-old sister Merry half to death when I came home from church one night. I told her, "Mom and Dad better vote for Reagan or else all the children will be rounded up in concentration camps and made into slaves by Mondale, because he's the Antichrist." I showed her the tract I received at church to prove it.

Merry ran to our parents' room crying hysterically and slobbering all over her pj's. She begged them to vote for Reagan. Understand, in the mid- to late 1960s our mother was a member of the Philadelphia chapter of the Student Nonviolent Coordinating Committee (SNCC) at the time that Stokely Carmichael was chairman. When I handed her the tract, my mother was stupefied.

She pressed me, "Where did you get this?"

"From church," I punched back, "so it must be true!"

She threatened to take me out of that church, but I countered, "You can take the girl out of the church, but you can't take the church out of the girl!"

She never did take me out of that church.

From that point on, my relationship with my mother and the rest of my family was strained. They felt like they lost me to an adopted family they didn't know or understand. My Wesleyan pastor, Rev. Campbell, reached out to my mother, but the gulf between them was too wide. When I switched to the white United Methodist Church across the tracks, things got worse instead of better. The tendency of many American teenagers is to distance themselves from their parents and become peer oriented. My peers were white evangelicals and my world began to revolve around friends, not family. Also, my family at home was a blended family with challenges of its own. Both my mother and stepfather, who later adopted me, had children when they married. The difficulty of integrating two families led me to seek the stability of my adopted evangelical family. As my evangelical faith increased, it also separated me from my African American family and surrounding community. I heard only one thing from my white Christian friends about politics. Christians are Republican. I believed it—until an experience in college began to raise questions.

My undergraduate years at Rutgers University coincided with the late Reagan years and with three major American cultural phenomena: the increased occurrence of homeless families and children, the increase in AIDS consciousness, and the rise of the Religious Right and the Christian Coalition. The Right's ascent was most visible through massive pro-life protests on college campuses.

Beginning my first year on campus, I became deeply involved in Campus Crusade for Christ, a conservative evangelical ministry to college students. I was a student leader who attended every retreat, every leadership conference, and went on my first mission trip the summer after my freshman year to learn how to do evangelism more effectively. I joined pro-life rallies on campus with my friends and attended counterprotests when pro-choice demonstrations marched through the center of the campus.

During the summer between my junior and senior years, though, I went on a second mission project. Campus Crusade was in the midst of developing a new ministry with an urban focus called Here's Life Inner City. The stated purpose of this particular Summer in the City project in New York was to give students "God's eyes to view the city."

My team partnered with the Times Square Church soup kitchen, where I met Johnny, a self-identified "wino" and Korean War vet who wept when we offered to help him up the stairs to get a bowl of soup. Johnny lived in a doorway near the Port Authority Bus Terminal. I visited him there every day for two weeks, during which we saw Johnny come to life as he told stories of his previous life. Leaving Johnny was like leaving family. Next my team spent a week at Camp Comanche, a camp for at-risk youth, almost all of them African American. The youth reminded me of my friends from the block on Walnut Lane in the West Oak Lane section of Philadelphia, where I lived until I was eight years old.

John Perkins's *With Justice for All* was required reading on the project. It introduced me to the effects of racism and systemic injustice among my people and helped me see beyond the degradation and violence of ghettoized neighborhoods. By the time the summer was over I saw Johnny and the youth of Camp Comanche from a new perspective. I saw their intrinsic beauty and their infinite worth. I did indeed see them through God's eyes and, as a result, something more profound happened. My view of myself began to change.

Johnny and the Camp Comanche kids were the first African American people I'd had consistent personal contact with, besides my own family, since moving away from Philadelphia in grade school. That summer, as I saw Johnny and the kids through God's eyes, I began to see myself reflected back. I saw my own intrinsic beauty and my own infinite worth.

That Summer in the City was a healing season. For the first time since I became an evangelical Christian, I saw that God cared for my people. I returned to Rutgers excited to share my newfound sense of justice grounded in faith. I joined the campus group RU with the Homeless, a small group with a big name and profile. We started a homeless shelter just off campus. We took turns spending the night at the shelter and did whatever we could to help keep it afloat. I became a worship leader, based on my assumption that homeless people need food for the soul as much as they need food for their stomachs. I was already the leader of the Campus Crusade worship team, a relatively progressive subgroup within a larger conservative community. We were all friends anyway, so when I asked they jumped at the chance to help out. The team led worship for the men at the shelter every Sunday night.

A clash of worldviews within Campus Crusade, however, became obvious. At a regular meeting during the announcements time, a student entreated everyone to join him at an Operation Rescue antiabortion rally that weekend. After he sat down, I stood up and invited the students also to join the worship team at the homeless shelter that Sunday. After the meeting, the Operation Rescue participant came up to me and said, "Homelessness is the world's issue. Abortion is God's issue." He insinuated that I needed to get in line with God and drop my "worldly" concerns. That conversation was the beginning of the end of my life as a developing Republican. Here a conservative evangelical organization had reintroduced me to my people and showed me that God cares for the poor and, therefore, I should care. Yet the overwhelming witness of my Republican evangelical community was that God did not care, so I should not.

That same year, the AIDS quilt stopped at Rutgers on its tour around the world, and it served to deepen my compassion for others. As I walked the rows of patchwork memorials, I found myself looking for the panel for Jimmy, who had been my childhood hairdresser. My mother had called recently to tell me, "Jimmy died of AIDS." His death and the quilt made personal to me the impact of AIDS and the condition of the gay community, which bore the brunt of the epidemic. The quilt was another small point of departure from the evangelical Republican Party line that AIDS was God's punishment of gays.

In August 1990, I moved to New York City. At the same time, about seven other Campus Crusade alumni/ae from the Summer in the City project also arrived in the city. I worked for the off-Broadway Lamb's Theatre Company, founded by members of the Lamb's Church of the Nazarene. I lived on the sixth floor above the theater with boarders who worked for the church. It was there, at the Lamb's Church, that I wrote my first play about a born-again Christian who confronted her own lack of compassion for the oppressed. It was also at the church that I met my first real-life, born-again Democrat. He was from Los Angeles.

SHIFTING WORLDS AND VIEWS

Since then, my political leanings, as with many evangelicals of my generation, have undergone a shift. I moved to Los Angeles in 1991 to attend the Bresee Institute for Urban Mission, a satellite campus for seminaries without access to urban centers, developed by the Los Angeles First Church of the Nazarene. Phineas F. Bresee, who founded the Church of the Nazarene denomination in 1895 on skid row in Los Angeles, proclaimed a simple yet profound theology: "There is no holiness without social holiness!" At the Bresee Institute and at the Los Angeles First Church of the Nazarene, people were spread across the political spectrum. There were Republicans, Democrats, and independents. I was most fascinated by the Democrats: "Is it possible to be a Christian and a Democrat?" I wondered. Their presence offered me informal permission to embrace my family's Democratic roots for the first time since I had become a born-again follower of Jesus.

In those California years, the physical distance from my family was vast. Despite the three thousand miles between us, the gap between my mother and me began to close. When I told stories of my work with at-risk youth at the Bresee Youth Center, she could understand. When I shared stories of my life as an advocate for the poor, she connected to that kind of faith.

Later, as director of ethnic reconciliation for InterVarsity Christian Fellowship (IVCF) of Greater Los Angeles from 1999 to 2004 and as Southern California ethnic reconciliation specialist from 2004 to 2005, I witnessed InterVarsity's shift. It was a transformation within one of the largest and oldest collegiate parachurch ministries in the United States. InterVarsity's shift was not a political one. It was a shift in worldview, what some call theology. As InterVarsity invested deeply in the process of becoming a racially reconciling organization, its theology broadened to embrace the worldviews of the organization's staff and students of color as well as women. That theological shift brought transformation from the inside out. It led key leaders in InterVarsity to question the very nature of the gospel it had been proclaiming on campus. Beginning in 1990, InterVarsity's perception of the gospel moved from a limited message, focused exclusively on individual sin and salvation, toward a vision of a transformed world, focused on the good news of the coming of the kingdom of God.

This good news inspires work toward a world where justice and mercy roll down together into a mighty stream. It guides the journey toward a world where all the relationships in creation are brought back into right relationship with each other. A vibrant peace will prevail between people and God, men and women, families, ethnic groups, nations, and humans and the rest of creation, and oppressive systems and structures will be transformed to serve humanity and help each person thrive. The Bible captures this kind of world in the word *shalom* (holistic peace). Shalom is what the kingdom of God smells, tastes, feels, and looks like. It is justice, peace, mercy, reciprocity, harmony, integrity, beauty, truth telling, restoration, and reparation, just for starters.

InterVarsity's theology or worldview is stretching to encompass this broad understanding of the good news. That stretch is making an impact on the way the organization communicates the gospel to college campuses. InterVarsity reaches approximately thirty thousand college and university students each year. IVCF alumni are making an impact in the public square and in churches.

In the fall of 2006, I witnessed another door opening to a new evangelical movement. I became a featured writer for the Christian blog FaithfulDemocrats.com. I will never forget our first day on the Web. We were a Christian community "coming out of the political closet," so to speak. We discovered that we could say the unspeakable out loud without shame or fear of exorcism from the evangelical family. We were evangelicals, and we were Democrats. This seemed revolutionary at the time, not because the norm of evangelicalism was shifting from Republican to Democrat, but because, up to that point, it was still widely assumed that to be an evangelical meant to be a Republican. We broke that mold. Now it has burst wide open.

In late 2007, when Jim Wallis stood on the stage of Hostos Community College in the South Bronx in front of an audience of three hundred, my family was there. They drove two and a half hours from South Jersey to be a part of the launch of a faith-based antipoverty movement in New York City called NY Faith & Justice, which had selected me to direct it. There was evangelical worship. A government official, also a member of a prominent church in the city, admonished the gathering to be active in the public arena. Members from an array of church traditions and ethnicities offered prayers. I spoke about the vision of Isaiah 61 as the fuel that drove this new movement. Then Wallis took the stage and spoke; many who heard him were unaware that the Christian faith could be connected to public action.

When the last guest filed out, my mother, dad, sister, brother-in-law, and niece remained with me and core members of NY Faith & Justice. My parents surprised me. They focused on Jim Wallis, a white evangelical Christian. They liked him. They found it hard to believe they liked him, but they liked him nonetheless. They talked about Wallis's call to "personal faith that is never private" the whole way home in the car. My family has since given their blessing to my faith and my ministry. My mother shares her stories of organizing with SNCC in Philadelphia, telling me how she worked to find Philadelphia churches willing to partner with SNCC "back in the day."

My story is just one example of the story of evangelicals of my generation. We are undergoing a fundamental transformation that is loosening the Republican Party's tightly held grip on evangelical America since Ronald Reagan's bid for the presidency in 1980. This spiritual reformation has profound public consequences.

RACE, POLITICS, AND RELIGION

It has been said the most segregated hour in America is from eleven to twelve o'clock on Sunday mornings. In that hour Americans divide by race and split off into separate places of worship. Michael Emerson and Christian Smith, who have studied evangelicals and the problem of race in America, contend that evangelical religion and its conduct in the United States have divided America. Their research has led them to assert that the deepest racial divide in the United States is between the worldviews of black and white evangelicals. These competing worldviews pit white evangelicals, who overwhelmingly tend to align with the Republican Party, against black evangelicals, who overwhelmingly support the Democratic Party.[4]

Emerson and Smith explain these splits using the theory of "cultural tool kits," originally developed by sociologist Ann Swidler. Affiliated groups of people use cultural tool kits to interpret the world. A group's tools are limited by the experiences of its members, and its shared set of tools limits its members' abilities to interpret the world, integrate information, and adapt to change. They argue that white evangelical cultural tool kits perpetuate the problem of racism in America, albeit often unwittingly.

After conducting two thousand phone interviews with black and white evangelicals, Emerson and Smith found three distinct tools in the white evangelical tool kit. First is the belief that humans exist outside the control of structures and institutions and are therefore accountable for their individual actions independent of context. Emerson and Smith called this tool "accountable freewill individualism." The second tool, "relationalism," involved attaching primary importance to interpersonal relationships. Finally, the third tool was an inability to perceive or unwillingness to accept the influence of social structures, which they called "anti-structuralism."[5] This cultural tool kit leaves the vast majority of white evangelicals unable to grasp the impact of social structures and institutions on individuals; it supports an historical worldview that believes the individual is free from the influence of history; and it allows people to ignore how they are responsible for being historical actors.[6]

While black evangelicals shared this white evangelical tool kit, Emerson and Smith's survey of them uncovered two additional tools: (1) the ability to perceive and accept the influence of social structures, called "structuralism," and (2) the ability to perceive the influence of history in the present, called "historical worldview." These tools were also present to varying degrees among white evangelicals if they were immersed in a network of relationships with African Americans that went well beyond a few interpersonal friendships. Those extra tools made all the difference. The absence of them among most white evangelicals inhibited their ability to comprehend the importance of systemic/institutional oppression.[7]

There is truth and tragedy in the old saying that the most segregated hour in America is Sunday morning. The homogenous, insular way evangelical congregations are structured in the United States creates the perfect system for perpetual replication of limited tool kits within white evangelical communities. Hence, Emerson and Smith conclude that, given that three-quarters of Americans identified themselves as evangelicals at the time *Divided by Faith* was published in 2000, the only remedy for the race problem in America is the desegregation of the evangelical congregational structure.[8]

Emerson and Smith's research shows it is not enough for white evangelicals to have a few African American, Latino, Native American, or Asian American friends. To transform the white evangelical worldview, their church members must be immersed in communities of color or a network of friends of color. In a follow-up study, *United by Faith*, the various authors used historical, theological, and sociological evidence to illuminate the need for congregational desegregation and integration. They also discussed processes for effecting such changes.[9]

Emerson and Smith stopped their study at the race line. I take it one step further by asking a simple question: is there a relationship between political worldview and theological worldview? While politics were not the focus of Emerson and Smith's theory, it lurked in the background: they discovered that the deepest divide in worldview in the country is not just between whites and blacks. It is between white and black *evangelicals*. It is understandable, then, that these two groups tend to vote overwhelmingly for opposing political parties, because *worldview* is ultimately what we're talking about. Both politics and theology are ultimately about the one comprehensive worldview a group holds. People vote and people worship according to their worldviews.

Worldview shapes both politics and worship. Hence, white evangelical politics and the white evangelical theological worldview are closely related. One theological worldview led white evangelicals to adopt the Republican Party as its own. Today, a theological worldview *shift* is loosening the alignment between Republicans and evangelicals. This book is the story of that shift.

The evangelical worldview shapes one's understanding of the gospel to a great degree. While progressive or liberal

Christians gain their perspective of the world utilizing several resources, including scripture, tradition, history, science, philosophy, personal experience, and current context, evangelicals (white or black) tend to believe in the prime authority of the scriptures. Thus, most evangelicals would say their worldview conforms to the truth as revealed in the scriptures. In other words, they would say their cultural tool kits are determined by their biblically based faith.

In actuality, however, it might be more accurate to say their kits determine how they read the Bible, and the prime importance evangelicals accord to scripture makes how they interpret it crucial to understanding evangelical action or inaction in the world. I contend that what evangelicals see and use in scripture, what focuses their attention, what they omit, what they can comprehend, and what baffles them in scripture is filtered through the grid of (1) accountable freewill individualism, (2) relationalism, and (3) antistructuralism. As a result, the white evangelical perception of the gospel has been truncated by a limited cultural tool set and guided by the obsession of Religious Right leaders, who focus on two issues of personal morality—gay marriage and abortion—to the exclusion of structural and systemic sin.

This cultural limitation was the case throughout the twentieth century, but in the twenty-first century evangelicals are adding more tools to their kit. Increased contact with a browning America are challenging their limited worldviews. In addition, with the rise of global people's liberation movements in the 1960s through the 1990s, dominant power groups were confronted with views of truth from the underside of oppression. White evangelicals came face to face with views of Jesus's good news from the perspective of the poor, the oppressed, and the vulnerable. These alternative views challenged and stretched white evangelical understandings of Jesus and his earthly mission.

In this book, I tell the story of evangelical America as I have experienced it and as sixty-seven established and emerging evangelical leaders have related the story to me through interviews. I begin with the roots of American evangelical faith and the great divorce that split the American church at the turn of the twentieth century, then turn to the mid-twentieth-century prophets who called evangelical America back to its roots and laid the foundations for its twenty-first-century return to a commitment to a better world. Three case studies, the Promise Keepers, the Southern Baptist Convention, and InterVarsity Christian Fellowship, illustrate a range of organizational responses to the evangelical prophets throughout the latter half of the twentieth century. Finally, I turn to the outcome of the tectonic shift and examine what is "new" about the good news that evangelicals are embracing and how this new perspective on the gospel affects evangelical politics and activism.

This shift, while appearing political, is, at heart, deeper and longer lasting than partisan politics. In these pages I will show how evangelical does not equal Republican or Democrat. Political parties do not exist to call forth the kingdom of God. They exist to perpetuate themselves and hold on to power. Evangelical once equaled, and is coming to equal again, people aligned with Jesus, and Jesus aligns himself with the least in society. Those who claim to follow him must believe, as Shane Claiborne has said, "Another world is possible. Another world is necessary." [10]

From our earliest beginnings, evangelicals have not only believed another world is necessary, we have worked to make it possible. In the days of the antebellum South, enslaved men and women believed in and struggled for another world, escaping north to freedom. From generation to generation they told stories of resistance and hope. Though many died in captivity, they believed that one day their descendants would dance unfettered in freedom land. In the physical sense, freedom land was synonymous with the North and Canada—the land where the law protected the right of self-determination. In a spiritual sense, freedom land was a land of truth, liberty, justice and mercy, reparation, redemption, restoration, and vindication. Freedom land was also heaven for those who had gone before. As I survey the shake-up within evangelical America, I see evangelicals heeding Jesus's call to work with him, intercede with him, weep with him, and wade with him through the muck and mire of *both* personal sin *and* systemic oppression here on earth. Jesus declares that he has come to set the captives free, and a new generation of evangelicals is committing its heart, mind, soul, and strength to walk with him to bring forth the kingdom of God on earth—as it is in heaven—to bring forth freedom land.

Roots, Fruits, and Mutants

Once, evangelicals helped change the world. In the 1800s, they fought against slavery. They fought against poverty. They fought for workers' rights and led the charge to form labor unions. They fought against slum housing. They even laid foundations for the fight for women's suffrage. *That* is the evangelical heritage, and it draws from deep progressive values grounded in the gospel.

In the years before the Civil War, the great evangelist Charles Finney designed the first altar calls with a twofold purpose. People walked forward to accept Jesus as their savior *and* to sign up for the abolitionist movement—both at the same time! He "insisted as late as 1868, 'the loss of interest in benevolent enterprises' was usually evidence of a 'backslidden heart.' "[1]

These are evangelical roots, so why are so many Christians skittish today about the moniker "evangelical"? Many of the evangelical leaders I interviewed felt uncomfortable with the term because, as they put it, "It means something different now." "It means fundamentalist." "It means Religious Right." It means only caring about two issues, and that's it: abortion and sexual morality. "And that's not me," they protested in chorus. The mainstream media, which do not understand this evangelical heritage, have bought the hype of the Religious Right, which has dubbed itself the true evangelical Christians. But this recent hype distorts evangelical roots and creates a serious mismatch between the dominant forms of evangelicalism that have emerged over the past thirty years and the evangelical roots of yesteryear. The fruit of the Religious Right is not fruit of the evangelical tree. Maybe it is a special breed or genetic mutant. But it did not grow from the same Finney tree.

Many of my interviewees said they no longer call themselves evangelicals publicly. *But*, they insisted defiantly, if we are talking about evangelical roots—the evangelicalism of the nineteenth century—then, "Yes, I'm an evangelical!" When I asked them, "How do you define 'evangelical'?" I usually got an incredulous, "Can anyone define 'evangelical' nowadays?" But when pressed to try, the interviewees, with few exceptions, consciously or unwittingly used British historian David W. Bebbington's definition.

Bebbington identified evangelicals as ones who had passionate commitments to four dimensions of Christian faith: biblicism, conversionism, crucicentrism, and activism. Biblicism grounds faith in scripture as authoritative. Conversionism emphasizes the reality of the newness of life faith in Christ brings. Crucicentrism confesses that Christ's work on Calvary redeems all of life. Finally, activism is how faith in the newness of life, which Christ gives believers, is lived through everyday efforts. In addition to an increased concern for sharing the faith, this last dimension led some evangelicals to advance abolition, suffrage, emancipation for the oppressed, and civil rights. When evangelicals became missionaries they did not simply talk about the gospel; they tried to stop foot binding in China, they built schools for girls in Asia, they opposed dowries and sati—the burning of widows—in India, and founded hospitals where there were none.[2]

RECLAIMING "EVANGELICAL"

Words mean too much to let them be hijacked when they have such deep, important roots. To give up the moniker "evangelical"—to let it be changed to mean something entirely different from its history—is not just a matter of semantics. To let the Religious Right define evangelical obscures an entire era of American history. It erases the memory of real people who lived and fought for just causes and social policies *because* of their faith . . . because of the faith I now hold. I refuse to let the Religious Right confiscate my heritage. I am an evangelical and proud of it. I know our history, and I know our roots are deep and life giving.

My mother embarked on a genealogical search for our family roots. She traced her mother's lineage back to the last adult slave in our family. Leah Ballard had seventeen children and five husbands because her families kept being sold away. My mother traced her father's side back to the Cherokee Trail of Tears. His ancestors escaped the trail in Kentucky and listed themselves as white on the 1840 census. They were not white. We have pictures. For good measure, my mother made me watch *Roots* every time it aired from 1977 through late 1986 (the year I went off to college). I probably saw it twenty times. I know my roots and the country's roots.

I have been thinking about spiritual roots lately. Ethnic roots reveal the ways family trees and whole ethnic groups were shaped and formed by the forces of history. In like manner spiritual roots reveal how current-day faith is also grounded in the past. Both sides of my mother's spiritual roots flow from the Anglican heritage found in the black Episcopal church tradition. My family's spiritual forebearers can be traced back to Absalom Jones and Richard Allen.

The first black Episcopal church was born in 1792 when Jones and Allen attempted to pray at the altar in a segregated Episcopal church in Philadelphia. White ushers dragged the two men from the altar, and the blacks in the galleries followed in mass protest. Two years later, St. Thomas African Episcopal Church was established as part of the Episcopal Diocese of Pennsylvania. Jones, the first black ordained minister of any denomination in the United States, was appointed the priest of the congregation in 1802.[3] Allen went on to found the distinct and historically black African Methodist Episcopal denomination.

When my mother's maternal grandmother moved north from South Carolina in the 1920s, she settled in South Philadelphia where she joined St. Simon the Cyrenian Episcopal Church, a historically black congregation in her neighborhood. When my mother's paternal grandfather moved to Philadelphia around the same time, his wife and children joined St. Mary's Church near Center City, another historically black Episcopal church. On both sides, my ancestors attended church on and off through the years, always inspired by the good news of liberation for the oppressed.

Black Episcopalians hold a special place in the heritage of the black church in America. At a time when African Americans founded separate black denominations, the black Episcopalians never separated from the larger Episcopal denomination. Instead, they founded separate congregations, living in the tension between their quest for self-determination and their attempt at racial reconciliation within a white denomination. The Episcopal Church was one of the richest denominations in the United States in the nineteenth century, and its parishioners held more slaves than any other American denomination. In the face of this white privilege, black Episcopalians spoke prophetically to their white slave-holding counterparts, calling on them to heed the good news of Jesus's liberation of the oppressed. On January 1, 1808, the day the 1807 Slave Trade Act took effect in the United States, abolishing the transatlantic slave trade, Absalom Jones preached a sermon entitled "A Thanksgiving Sermon." He denounced slavery and referenced the abolition of the British and American transatlantic slave trades as evidence that God the Father always acted on "behalf of the oppressed and distressed."[4]

I was baptized Episcopalian at St. Luke's Church in the Germantown section of Philadelphia in 1974. Soon after, though, my family lost contact with the church when we moved from Philadelphia, a black Episcopal haven, to Cape May, New Jersey, which was no haven for anything black.

I found faith again in the evangelical Wesleyan and United Methodist churches in Cape May. The forebearers of my adopted white evangelical heritage include John Wesley, William Wilberforce, and Charles Finney. Many evangelicals look back to these founders to ground their spiritual heritage, but not just to these white male forebearers. Some also turn to Phoebe Palmer, Sojourner Truth, and Harriet Beecher Stowe, as well as the editors of the Baptist *Watchman and Reflector* newspaper. They brandished their words for the causes of abolition and women's rights. In addition, Phineas F. Bresee and Henry Clay Fish pressed for economic empowerment for the poor and downward mobility for the rich.

My spiritual roots, like my ethnic roots, are diverse. The faith of all my spiritual ancestors—like that of most evangelicals today—can be traced to an array of eighteenth- and nineteenth-century faith leaders on at least two continents, from various ethnic backgrounds and denominations, both women and men. Their faith in Jesus compelled them to fight for justice. They are my "cloud of witnesses" (Hebrews 12:1). The Jesus-followers described in this chapter demonstrated evangelical faith that inspires me to press on to gain the prize for which I have been called . . . the redemption of our world and the coming of freedom land.

EVANGELICAL ANCESTRAL ROOTS

John Wesley (1703–1791), an Anglican clergyman and Christian theologian, advocated the ancient church idea of the spiritual perfectability of humanity, what he called "Christian Perfectionism." This idea became a key foundation for the Christian revivals and reform movements of the nineteenth century. He called believers to personal, interpersonal, and societal holiness. That holiness would be manifest in the form of perfect love. A Wesleyan journal, *Zion's Herald*, helped ignite a social justice movement by communicating Christian Perfectionism to the masses. In 1854 the journal's editor called Christians to overthrow slavery, intemperance, political corruption, and all other public vices because commitment to Christ must be lived out through both personal and social morality.[5]

The belief that we are called to love perfectly and pursue holiness of heart and life here and now became part and parcel of the revival movement that swept America following the 1858 Fulton Street Revival in New York City. As a result, followers of Wesley fought against child labor and for many social reforms that would help the poor and exploited.

In 1791, the year of his death, John Wesley wrote his last letter to William Wilberforce (1759–1833), urging him to continue his fight against the British slave trade:

> Unless the divine power has raised you us [*sic*] to be as *Athanasius contra mundum*, I see not how you can go through your glorious enterprise in opposing that execrable villainy which is the scandal of religion, of England, and of human nature. Unless God has raised you up for this very thing, you will be worn out by the opposition of men and devils. But if God be for you, who can be against you? Are all of them together stronger than God? O be not weary of well doing! Go on, in the name of God and in the power of his might, till even American slavery (the vilest that ever saw the sun) shall vanish away before it.
>
> Reading this morning a tract wrote by a poor African, I was particularly struck by that circumstance that a man who has a black skin, being wronged or outraged by a white man, can have no redress; it being a "law" in our colonies that the oath of a black against a white goes for nothing. What villainy is this?[6]

Wilberforce had decided to follow Jesus in 1784. In subsequent years, Wilberforce's faith and the outworking of that faith would impact the world.

Soon after his conversion, Wilberforce became racked

by the question of whether he could serve God and his nation in Parliament. John Newton, the former slave-ship captain who wrote "Amazing Grace," told Wilberforce God had raised him up for such a time as this.

In 1789, when he was thirty years old, Wilberforce partnered with Quaker abolitionists and Olaudah Equiano (ca. 1745–1797), a free Christian African who wrote an eyewitness account of his life as a slave. With this new coalition, Wilberforce brought the fight to the House of Commons. Wilberforce spent twenty years of his life fighting for the abolition of the British slave trade, an industry as commonplace and profitable in his world as the technology industry is in ours. In his first speech to Parliament, he read for three hours fact after fact about the evils of slavery and then challenged his fellow lawmakers: "Having heard all of this you may choose to look the other way, but you can never again say that you did not know."[7] His public pressure campaign yielded its fruit on February 23, 1807, at 4 o'clock in the morning when the Commons voted 283 to 16 to abolish the British slave trade.

Wilberforce is best known as the leader of the British abolitionist movement, but his faith led him to work against many forms of human degradation, as have the Methodist movements John Wesley inspired. He organized for education reform, an end to child labor, health-care reform, and prison reform. An evangelical to the core, he worked to ensure that human beings were treated with the dignity and respect deserving of those bearing the image of God, and according to his evangelical faith, all human beings bore that image.

In the mid-nineteenth century's Second Great Awakening, religious fervor swept the United States from Maine south to the Carolinas and west to the Mississippi. Known as perhaps its greatest revival preacher, Charles Finney (1792–1875) crafted the evangelical framework for social reform. He believed Christian discipleship should influence the way Christians interacted with God and with the social world around them, so he paired spiritual revival with social engagement. Finney's revivals won converts to Christianity and to the movement to abolish U.S. slavery. Slave owners could not be true Christians, according to Finney. He was one of the first to prohibit slaveholders from taking communion. While Finney never thought of himself primarily as a reformer, his mass revivals became the vehicle through which reform movements spread, gained public support, and eventually influenced public policy throughout the 1800s.

Early in the women's suffrage movement, Phoebe Palmer (1807–1874) worked to establish women's religious rights using the authority of the Holy Spirit: "And it shall come to pass in the last days, saith God, I will pour out my spirit upon all flesh: and your sons and your daughters shall prophesy" (Acts 2:17). Her 1858 book, *Promise of the Father; or a Neglected Specialty of the Last Days*, broke ground for women's religious rights. It spoke to evangelical leaders across the country who believed leadership granted by the gifts of the Spirit was reserved for men. Through her reading of the Bible, she convinced some of these leaders that women had indeed been granted gifts of the Spirit and that there was a legitimate leadership role for women in the revival meetings of the nineteenth century. Palmer's contemporaries were the likes of Harriet Beecher Stowe, whom she consulted on the draft of her book, and Charles Finney, with whom she partnered often in revival meetings.

Harriet Beecher Stowe (1811–1896) was raised in an

evangelical family. Her father, Lyman Beecher, was a renowned abolitionist preacher who used his Congregational-
ist pulpit in Connecticut to advocate for Missouri's entrance
into the Union as a free state in 1820. Beecher Stowe used
her talent as a writer to live out her family's commitment to
abolition. Her book *Uncle Tom's Cabin* harnessed the power
of narrative to expose the hidden evil of slavery in the United
States. Her book not only galvanized the evangelical masses,
it also ignited public sentiment against slavery. According to
legend, President Lincoln once credited her book as the
force "that started the Civil War."[8]

Isabella Baumfree, a.k.a. Sojourner Truth (ca. 1797–
1883), was the youngest daughter of Mau-mau Bett, an enslaved woman whose parents came from the coast of
Guinea.[9] Baumfree's paternal grandmother was a Mohawk
woman. Baumfree and her youngest brother, Peter, remained with their mother when each of their siblings was
sold away. In the evenings, when the day's trials were done,
Baumfree's mother stared at the stars and saw the ten older
children she had lost. In her mind's eye, each star held
the face of a daughter or son. She would call her children to
her and talk to them in the heavens.

"My children, there is a God, who hears and sees you,"
Mau-mau explained.

"A *God*, Mau-mau! Where does he live?" asked her heavenly children.

"He lives in the sky," Mau-mau replied, "and when you
are beaten, or cruelly treated, or fall into any trouble, you
must ask help of him, and he will always hear and help you."[10]

Mau-mau's deep Christian faith inspired Isabella's own
lifelong faith commitments. That faith led her to become one
of the most renowned and controversial activist preachers of

her time. An abolitionist and women's rights advocate, Baumfree is now legend. Her picture even graces the face of a U.S. postage stamp. Yet most people don't know about the deep faith that guided her life's work.

Baumfree was enslaved by Dutch owners in southeastern New York. She had several owners throughout her childhood, some extremely cruel. Isaac S. and Maria Van Wagener, a Quaker couple, bought and freed her. As a free woman, Isabella was amazed one day when God's presence filled the room. She said God showed her that he filled everything, the entire universe. There was nowhere she could go where God was not. "I jes' walked round an' round in a dream," Baumfree said to Harriet Beecher Stowe when she explained her conversion experience. "Jesus loved me! I knowed it, I felt it."[11]

That conversion changed Isabella's life forever. She believed that God gave her a new name and a new mission. She would be Sojourner Truth: "Sojourner" because God was calling her to travel around the northeast states, "showing the people their sins and be a sign unto them," and "Truth" because she was to tell the truth about the horrors of enslavement.[12] Sojourner Truth became an itinerant preacher whose six-foot presence halted crowds and commanded their attention. She preached the truth of slavery to crowds who threw stones and food at her at first; but when she opened her mouth, they listened with rapt attention.

Two books stayed close to Sojourner throughout her life. One she called her *Book of Life*. Abraham Lincoln signed it in 1864: "To Aunty Sojourner Truth. —A. Lincoln." The other book was her Bible. Baumfree's free children read her passages from the text each night until her passing in 1883. Though she herself was not taught to read, others may now read the many books and plays that have been written about her life and work.

EVANGELICAL CONTRADICTIONS

There are other evangelicals who built the stage for evangelicalism. One was George Whitefield, often called the founder of American evangelicalism. In Whitefield we see a fuller picture of the contradictions of white evangelical faith and practice. As early as 1740, Whitefield fought for the intrinsic equality of blacks and whites and won the battle that opened access to the gospel to blacks. As a result, black men and women converted to Christianity in droves. Yet Whitefield also upheld the institution of slavery, even going so far as to say blacks needed slavery because "bondage was their best insurance of salvation." [13]

Michael Emerson and Christian Smith call attention to the mixed history of evangelical faith foundations in *Divided by Faith: Evangelical Religion and the Problem of Race in America*. They cite a number of examples of reforming revivalists of the eighteenth and nineteenth centuries, including Whitefield, Cotton Mather, and Charles Finney, who ultimately failed to understand the full implications of the fact that black men and women were made equally in the image of God. Their understanding of the gospel isolated spiritual salvation from social and material equality. In focusing on ultimate spiritual needs, they were able to separate the good news from social reform. They relegated social policies and political action to "worldly" concerns. For them the need to win converts always trumped the need for social reform. So, in each case, when push came to shove, they chose not to rock the majority white culture's boat and, in each case, slavery ultimately remained unaddressed.

This is a tragic reality in the evangelical heritage. It compels me to ask my evangelical ancestors across racial lines and across the barrier of time: *What gospel were you preaching? What happened to the good news that all human beings are made in the image of God and must receive the respect and protection due all who bear the image of the creator?*

Though they preached faith in Jesus Christ and went partway in living it out, they, like most people, were most protective of their privilege and power. Their failures indicate, perhaps, that the struggle of evangelical faith is how to see the log in our own eyes. The best mirror I know is the example of lesser-known evangelical reformers. They continue to demonstrate what it means to be a follower of Jesus, a believer in his word who proclaims the good news of the kingdom of God, *on earth as it is in heaven.*

A HOUSE DIVIDED

The story of U.S. evangelicalism is like the story of ancient Israel, one nation that was divided by civil war. If the 1800s were the time of evangelical growth through revivals and movements to build up society through personal and social transformation, then the 1900s were the time of a house divided by new alliances of power. In the first half of the twentieth century, infighting resulted in fractures, and in the second half of the century, a large wayward faction moved in the opposite direction from visions of freedom land, even as a smaller faction held to the old vision of the kingdom of God on earth.

The betrayals began as the twentieth century turned. It was the industrial era. Immigrants and former slaves streamed into the cities. They searched for work. They searched for housing. They searched for new beginnings. In these urban jungles, they could not raise food from the ground, so they became dependent on the employment systems of the new industrial complex. Labor laws were nonexistent. Poverty was rampant as newcomers fought for jobs. Factory work was bone-crushingly hard and dangerous. Women and children alike worked in sweatshops more than twelve hours per day. Foul policies coupled with foul politics meant it was sink or swim for all.

When Walter Rauschenbusch looked around his impoverished Hell's Kitchen neighborhood in New York City, where he was the struggling pastor of the Second German Baptist Church from 1886–1897, he saw the Protestant church lulled into complacency by the individualistic Victorian worldview of the times. He wrestled with the mind-set of the Christians of his day. For these Victorian Christians, individuals were the masters of their own fate. If they were poor, they were poor because they did not work hard enough.[14]

Rauschenbusch struggled to find the good news in the Bible for the indigent masses. In 1908, six years after taking a professorship at Rochester Theological Seminary, he reflected on his days in New York City and wrote *Christianity and the Social Crisis*. In it he explained that there is more to poverty than laziness; there is systemic oppression.

> There is certainly a great and increasing body of chronic wretchedness in our wonderful country. It is greatest where our industrial system has worked out

its conclusions most completely. Our national optimism and conceit ought not to blind us longer to the fact. Single cases of unhappiness are inevitable in our frail human life; but when there are millions of them, all running along well-defined grooves, reducible to certain laws, then this misery is not an individual, but a social matter, due to causes in the structure of our society and curable only by social reconstruction.[15]

Christians, Rauschenbusch explained, are called to transform these structures and systems, bringing them under submission to the will of God. And what is the will of God? It is to establish His reign of peace, prosperity, wholeness, and life on earth for all.

To read *Christianity and the Social Crisis* a century later, one would think Rauschenbusch was speaking directly to the evangelical church of today. In response to the pervasive individualistic culture of his times, Rauschenbusch's kingdom of God theology focused the salvation equation on the social, this-worldly dimensions of the gospel. He rejected the need for individual redemption in the afterlife: "It is not a matter of getting individuals into heaven," he said, "but of transforming the life on earth into the harmony of heaven."[16] Rauschenbusch's critics faulted his this-worldly salvation for throwing the baby out with the bathwater.

In 1909, Cyrus Ingerson Scofield decided to counter the social-gospel movement by creating his own version of the Bible, the Scofield Study Bible. He added footnotes to promote the premillennial, dispensationalist claims of a fledgling sect within American evangelicalism. Scofield's worldview called Christians to prepare for the impending judgment of Christ, which he believed was coming soon. This belief was no different from that of many evangelical reformers of the eighteenth and nineteenth centuries. Finney, Truth, Wilberforce, Palmer, and the rest believed that a principal call of the good news was the call to holiness or perfection. They understood holiness, however, as operating on two dimensions, personal and social. Thus, along with the individual pursuit of personal holiness, Jesus followers worked to conform social systems to God's standards of perfection in preparation for Christ's return. Scofield and his followers, on the other hand, narrowed the scope of holiness to include only the personal spiritual dimension. This led Scofield's followers to pit the pursuit of personal holiness against the pursuit of social holiness. As a result, they disengaged from the social concerns of this world in favor of a laserlike focus on personal holiness. The outcome of this narrow focus was faith communities characterized by the propensity to form enclaves that viewed themselves in opposition to an outside world that threatened the holiness of the enclave.[17]

To promote his direct assault on the social gospel, Scofield twisted the biblical text to support what would later be called fundamentalism. Soon, fundamentalism's purveyors declared the urgent need to hold onto "the five fundamentals" of the gospel: (1) the inerrancy of the scriptures, (2) the virgin birth and the deity of Jesus, (3) substitutionary atonement as a sacrifice for sin, (4) Jesus's bodily resurrection, and (5) the authenticity of Jesus's miracles.

Most evangelicals today would agree with at least four of these five propositions, but would strongly object to the idea that they are the only "fundamentals." The list says nothing of Jesus's life and ministry beyond his miracles. As well, most evangelicals would object to identification with the funda-

mentalist movement altogether. Though evangelicals generally believe in the authority of the scriptures, they balk at the
way Scofield and other fundamentalists violated their own
first fundamental of the gospel by twisting the scriptures and
adding to their meaning to promote a theological agenda.
Second, Jesus is the central figure of evangelicalism, but the
fundamentalist movement became distinguished by three
worldviews that together created a belief system that stood in
contrast to the teachings of Jesus himself.

First, fundamentalists espoused dispensationalism, the
belief that God's purposes and methods of justification are
different at different points in biblical history. A tenet of dis-
pensationalists is that the Mosaic law (i.e., the Ten Com-
mandments and the other laws of Moses) is no longer needed
and now stands in opposition to Christ. In other words, God
established the law to save his people from sin in the Old Testament, but Christ's death on the cross paid the penalty for
human sin, so humans are now saved by faith alone in a substitutionary justification. This radical division between the
two Testaments was opposed most directly by evangelical
theologians Dan Fuller and Dallas Willard.

In his book *The Unity of the Bible,* Fuller argued the
Bible is one unified story of God's pursuit of right relationship with his people. Both in the Hebrew Bible and in the
New Testament, faith and obedience are equivalent. Obedience to the Mosaic law required faith just as obedience to
Jesus's words in the Sermon on the Mount require faith. The
purpose of the cross and resurrection are to give Christ followers the power and ability to obey. So, in Fuller's estima-
tion, to say one followed Jesus without obedience to his
commands was impossible.[18]

Likewise, Willard blasted the notion of faith without

works in his treatise *The Divine Conspiracy*. He advocated the abolition of a simplistic understanding of salvation, which he compared to being "scanned" into heaven on the merits of "bar-code faith."[19] The only thing needed in this conception of salvation was the sinner's admission that he could not pay for his own sins and needed Jesus to pay the penalty. From that point on, the sinner is released from the debt of sin, stamped with the faith bar code, and guaranteed entry to heaven. In this conception, the words of Jesus in the Sermon on the Mount, Matthew 25, Luke 4, Luke 10, and John 13:34 hold no weight. They are only suggestions for life, not imperative commands. Willard poked fun at the belief that how we live our lives has nothing to do with faith. This view, according to Willard, leads to inactive faith wholly disconnected from the person of Jesus.

Second, the fundamentalists advocated premillennialism, the belief that Jesus will come back to take his followers to heaven before the onset of Armageddon. This fundamentalist belief that history will culminate in a worldwide war reinforced their basic belief that there was no hope for humanity or the things of this world. The imminence of Armageddon was softened by the notion of *the rapture*—the belief that Christians would be taken up by God before the onset of the war and that Jesus would establish his reign on earth for a thousand years at the completion of the war. Premillennialism reinforced the fundamentalist call to disengage from society. If the world is on a path to imminent destruction, social reform is a waste of effort and time. Personal transformation is all that matters. Today's fundamentalists who call themselves Christian Zionists, however, have twisted this expectation of global destruction into a perverse form of social engagement. They advocate and pray for war to incite Armageddon.

Finally, fundamentalists held to the principle of separatism: Jesus's followers should extricate themselves from worldly influences to live life in contrast to cultural norms. They developed enclaves because they believed that Jesus opposes culture, encouraging homeschooling and other means to avoid contaminating influences from the larger society.

These fundamentalist ideas worked in concert to distort the picture of Jesus and the purposes of God on earth today. This belief system is best demonstrated by the contemporary apocalyptic narratives of Hal Lindsey's *Late Great Planet Earth* (1972) and Tim LaHaye and Jerry Jenkins's thirteen-part *Left Behind* book series (1995–2007).

The fundamentalist movement took on a life of its own within American evangelicalism throughout the 1920s and beyond. In 1920 Rev. Curtis Lee Laws used the term "fundamentalist" for the first time. Dallas Theological Seminary was founded in 1924 by Lewis Sperry Chafer, a student of C.I. Scofield, and became the primary source of the spread of Scofield's dispensationalist theology throughout the first half of the twentieth century. In 1925 the Scopes "Monkey" Trial rocked the United States with fundamentalist claims that evolution is biblical heresy and shouldn't be taught in schools. In 1929 the fundamentalists left Princeton Theological Seminary to form Westminster Theological Seminary. Some evangelicals also adopted fundamentalist ideas. Focused on eternal salvation and the coming of a new earth and heaven, fundamentalists and conservative evangelicals retreated from social reform and involvement in politics. By the time World War II began, it was clear that American evangelicalism was broken. Two extreme theologies within white evangelicalism—the social gospel and the fundamentalist gospel—fueled movements that spun off from them. In many respects, race defined the twentieth century from beginning to end, yet white theologians were silent. They were silent during the great migration of blacks from southern plantations to northern ghettos at the turn of the twentieth century and the northern race riots that ensued as disenfranchised blacks crossed Irish picket lines in search of work. They were silent during the horrific rise of the Ku Klux Klan and the practice of lynching-as-sport and as a ritual of white racial bonding. They were silent about the racial hatred and separatism within the white churches of the era. In their history of evangelicals, Emerson and Smith surmise that a large number of evangelicals—85 percent of all evangelicals at the time and half the U.S. population—supported racist behavior and policies, either by their silence or their participation in racially motivated violence.[20]

Few, if any, white theologians were talking about racism, even though many Christians of the era sat in their pews on Sunday morning after attending lynching parties on Saturday night. A leading twentieth-century founder of black theology, James Cone, charges: "From Jonathan Edwards to Walter Rauschenbusch and Reinhold Niebuhr to the present, progressive white theologians, with few exceptions, write and teach as if they do not need to address the radical contradiction that racism creates for Christian theology."[21]

VOICES OF THE DISINHERITED

Into this white vacuum spoke African American theologians Howard Thurman and Martin Luther King Jr., whom Thurman influenced. Howard Thurman (1899–1981) was among the foremost proponents of racial reconciliation from the 1940s through the 1970s. His book *Jesus and the Disinherited* (1949) did an unusual thing for its time—it considered the cross and the one nailed to it from the perspective of the downtrodden. Thurman began his treatise: "Many and varied are the interpretations dealing with the teachings and the life of Jesus of Nazareth. But few of these interpretations deal with what the teachings and the life of Jesus have to say to those who stand, at this moment in human history, with their backs against the wall." [22]

In this seminal work, Thurman searched Jesus's life and found four basic principles by which Jesus—the disinherited one—lived:

> You must abandon your fear of each other and fear only God. You must not indulge in any deception and dishonesty, even to save your lives. Your words must be Yea–Nay; anything else is evil. Hatred is destructive to hated and hater alike. Love your enemy, that you may be children of your Father who is in heaven. [23]

A professor, theologian, and ordained Baptist minister influenced by systematic theology professor George Cross, Gandhi, and the Quaker Rufus Jones, Thurman saw unchecked cross-racial violence in his time that led to unchecked suffering within the black community. He called all those who said they believed in Jesus to follow their disinherited leader into the revolutionary practice of sacrificial love not just in words, but in actions.

In the late 1920s, Thurman distanced himself from the

soul-saving black evangelical tradition as he embraced the mystical tradition of the Quakers and eventually came under the tutelage of Gandhi. Clarence E. Hardy III, however, reveals the ongoing influence of the black evangelical impulse that gave birth to Thurman's faith. The first major conversions of Africans in the United States coincided with the Second Great Awakening. Thurman's commitment to divine providence and the necessity of experienced spirituality versus text-based doctrinal knowledge demonstrates enduring influences from his early black evangelical roots:

> Sensory experience has been an important marker for much of black religious tradition. Visions during conversion experiences, dreams, signs and symbolic emblems depicting all-seeing eyes, and the like, are all instances where visual imagery is meant to convey special spiritual knowledge.[24]

Like his revivalist forebearers, Thurman understood that the good news did not exist in a personal moral vacuum. The gospel should be applied to every facet of life—economic, political, social, and personal. His message most closely resembled Sojourner Truth's calls to full racial equality, not just the abolition of slavery. Thurman called for the end of racial fear, hatred, and deception.

Thurman put his theology to the test when he accepted a position as co-pastor of the San Francisco–based, multiracial Church for the Fellowship of All Peoples. His partnering pastor was Alfred G. Fisk, a white ordained Presbyterian minister with a vision for a truly integrated church. Thurman scholar Alton B. Pollard III explained that Thurman saw his church as an experimental opportunity to demonstrate that divisions of race, class, gender, age, and denomination could be overcome within a diverse community. The experiment was, by and large, a success, and its existence called into question the normative status of the racially divided American church.[25]

Thurman's work inspired Martin Luther King Jr.'s vision of the beloved community and the nonviolent civil rights movement of the 1950s and 1960s. James Cone places King squarely in the black church/black theological tradition,[26] while Gary Dorrien contends King belongs to Thurman's liberal theological tradition.[27] However, Peter Heltzel, in his upcoming historical exploration of evangelical theology, *Lion on the Loose*, argues King was influenced by three theological influences simultaneously—black theology, liberal theology, and evangelical theology. Heltzel believes that while the black church tradition is the strongest of the three cords and liberal theology colors King's early sermons, the influence of evangelical theology—most prominent in King's later discourse (1966–1968)—has gone largely unacknowledged.[28]

King used the power of imagery to lay deep theological foundations for the movement. In his "Letter from Birmingham Jail," King called Jesus an "extremist for love." The Christian relationship to him was to be personal and expressed "through caring for the least of these" (Matthew 25). When King spoke of the beloved community in his 1963 speech in Washington, DC, he was calling America to take on the character of the Acts 2–4 church. The multiethnic, multicultural, multilingual church in Acts, of men and women, young and old, and rich and poor, broke bread together, shared all things in common, and grew exponentially.

King and other leaders of the civil rights movement, such as Fannie Lou Hamer, John Louis, Ed King, and Medgar

Evers, drew inspiration from eighteenth- and nineteenth-century evangelical activism. They marched in the streets in mass public protests, like Wilberforce's movement to end the slave trade, and, like their forerunners, they held public meetings, which always included hymns and spirituals. Also, somebody always rose up to testify to the truth, the truth about the kingdom and God's purposes on earth. These spirited gatherings mirrored the mass meetings used to great effect by Sojourner Truth, Phoebe Palmer, and Charles Finney.

Then it all unraveled . . . again.

It was the evening of June 21, 1964. Michael Schwerner and Andrew Goodman, Jewish Congress of Racial Equality (CORE) activists from New York City, and James Earl Chaney, an African American CORE activist from Meridian, Mississippi, drove along Highway 19 into Neshoba County.[29] They stopped at the home of the Coles, a black family, to ask how they were after their church had been bombed just days before. Soon after leaving, the three were arrested and then released at 10:30 PM. They left, but the police pursued them at high speed. Deputy Sheriff Cecil Price stopped them again and turned the three over to the Klan. Schwerner, Chaney, and Goodman were driven to an abandoned dirt road where, one by one, they were assassinated, shot dead.

On the night of August 7, 1964, Dave Dennis stood at the pulpit of First Union Baptist Church in Meridian. Four days earlier, the bodies of Chaney, Goodman, and Schwerner had been found and exhumed from an earthen dam on a farm in Neshoba County. On this night, Dennis was shaking. He was a young leader in the Mississippi Freedom Summer Project. A member of the Student Nonviolent Coordinating Committee (SNCC), Dennis believed that nonviolent resistance would work, but these murders shook him to his core: "I'm sick and tired of going to memorials; I'm sick and tired of going to funerals. I've got a bitter vengeance in my heart tonight . . . and I'm not going to stand here and ask anybody here not to be angry." [30]

That was the beginning of another great retreat from the vision of the kingdom. The movement had come so close, but it slipped from reach as they lay the boys' bodies in the ground. Dennis's anger tapped a well of latent African American rage and resentment toward whites in the movement. The antagonisms of us versus them began to prevail between blacks and whites in the movement and soon after, SNCC voted to excise all white leaders. The black power movement was born and the vision of King's beloved community was swallowed up by the violence and confusion of the late 1960s.

Into this context, in the fall of 1969, John Perkins cried out to an audience of black townspeople in Mendenhall, Mississippi:

> We've been patient. We've waited for them to change but they ain't gon' change until we stand up and be men and women. Stand up and look them straight in the eyes and demand our freedom. I don't know about y'all, but me and these children done decided that we ain't going to take it any more. We ain't going to take being second-class citizens. The United States Declaration of Independence says, "We hold these truths to be self-evident, that all men are created equal." Well, I am a man and I'm ready to stand and be treated like one. [31]

2

Prophets in a Wilderness

*No one can serve two masters; for a slave will either hate
the one and love the other, or be devoted to the one and
despise the other. You cannot serve God and wealth.*

—Matthew 6:24

Once more unto the breach, dear friends. Once more . . .

—Shakespeare

The polemic of either/or was the mind-set through the
mid-twentieth century. A person was *either* a capital-
ist *or* a communist and *either* black *or* white. A Christian
believed in *either* Rauschenbusch's social gospel *or* Scofield's
fundamentalist gospel. White evangelicals wrote off King's
prophetic message as social gospel communist propaganda,
and Thurman was virtually unknown by white evangelical
America.

In the maelstroms of these polarizations rose John M.
Perkins. Standing on the Simpson County (Mississippi)
courthouse steps, he picked up the baton of the civil rights
era and cried out for the implementation of a gospel that
called for *both* social *and* personal reform. In fact, multiple

prophets with similar messages rose up and called evangelical America to embrace a *both/and* gospel in the years following the civil rights movement. Tom Skinner, Jim Wallis, Tony Campolo, and Ron Sider all called the church back to a gospel worthy of the glory of God. It took nearly thirty years for a new generation to heed their calls, but these evangelical prophets laid the groundwork for the current generation's perception of the good news.

In a recent interview, Andy Crouch, editor at a leading evangelical magazine, *Christianity Today*, said of John Perkins, "It is funny how little known his name is, but in terms of shaping American evangelicalism as it comes into the twenty-first century, he is right up there with . . . Billy Graham."[1] No other Christian has made as deep and pervasive an impact on evangelical perceptions of justice as Perkins. This chapter explores the prophetic voices that laid the basis for the current shift within evangelical America, with a particular focus on the story and impact of Perkins, whom many consider the father of the late-twentieth-century evangelical justice movement.

BOTH / AND

In the summer of 2003, I took a journey through the American South: ten states, over four weeks, in one bus, with twenty InterVarsity Christian Fellowship (IVCF) staff workers and their families. We were taking the maiden voyage of IVCF's Pilgrimage for Reconciliation. Our charge was to retrace the Cherokee Trail of Tears and the African experience from slavery through the civil rights era. Our goal was to understand the nature of biblical peace—what it took to break it and what it takes to make it. Three moments along the way came together to teach a deep truth about how peace was broken on U.S. soil.

The initial moment came with our first stop at Delonega, Georgia, the epicenter of the first American gold rush. Back in 1828, a Cherokee boy found gold on the land. Within a year white gold miners swarmed the territory. Our guide at the Delonega Gold Museum explained that miners showed up from all over the East. They literally camped in the back-yards of Cherokee families without asking permission. Soon the U.S. government simply granted the miners that Chero-kee land.

In the museum's documentary, the narrator touted the ingenuity of the miners, who used the latest technology. The film reported how the miners blasted the northern Georgia hills with high-powered water hoses to squeeze all traces of gold from the land. Pictures of proud miners flickered across the screen. Only one obligatory mention was made of the Cherokees whose land the miners desecrated after they lob-bied Congress to steal it. The narrator simply said the Chero-kee people lived there.

The second moment happened in Montgomery, Al-abama, in the Rosa Parks Museum. Fascinated, I scanned the original documents from the bus boycott that sparked the modern civil rights movement. The documents lined the walls. I stopped dead in my tracks when I came to one hang-ing in the middle of one wall. It was a full-page newspaper ad—a letter from the White Citizens' Council to the "ne-groes" of Montgomery. The White Citizens' Council was or-ganized to protect the southern "way of life," or segregation. The letter called on blacks to stop the violence against their city! Over and over again, the word "violence" was repeated. The council called the bus boycott a "violent" act. I was dumbstruck. What is so "violent" about *not* getting on a bus? Did the council not consider the bombs they threw into the homes of Martin Luther King Jr. and Reverend Abernathy and into four black Baptist churches "violent"? What allowed the council to ignore such acts but to frame *not* getting on a bus as violent? My knees buckled when it hit me—it was the money. Montgomery's bus company lost three thousand fares per day for the duration of the boycott. It almost put the bus company out of business. So, there it was. When the boycott affected the bank accounts of those who benefited from the current system—*that economic boycott* was considered "violent."

The final moment of truth came at the very last stop on the journey. I had already been to the Martin Luther King Center in Atlanta, Georgia, so I gave the lobby a cursory once-over as others in our group studied the information on the walls. I glanced to my left and saw that a new exhibit had been mounted in the next room. "Okay," I thought. "Let's see what they have there."

As I approached the room, I saw that the walls were lined with paintings interspersed with dollar bills. A sign gave instructions: "Study the painting, then study the dollar bill next to it. See if you can find the picture from the painting in the dollar bill." The first painting carried the image of a happy slave, picking cotton and wearing a big grin. The dollar bill next to it carried a similar image. The same was true of the next painting and the next one after that. Scores of paintings lined these walls and each one had a dollar bill next to it that carried its image.

"What is the name of this exhibit?" I wondered.

I reached the end of the row and came across a plaque revealing the exhibit title, Confederate Currency: The Color of Money. These dollar bills were actual Confederate currency, produced after 1850 to rebut the rising abolitionist movement. The artist, John W. Jones, decided to focus on the pictures of happy slaves on the currency, reproducing it to reveal the way the Confederacy used currency as propaganda to justify the southern "way of life" to the rest of the world.

From these three pilgrimage moments, I learned a profound lesson. When money and maintaining a particular "way of life" become more important than the intrinsic dignity of humanity made in the image of God, we will desecrate the dignity of human beings and call all acts of resistance against oppression "violence." Peace will be plundered.

JOHN PERKINS: A CALL FROM THE COURTHOUSE STEPS

John M. Perkins stood on the steps of the Simpson County courthouse in 1969 after several months of failed boycotts. He persisted in his effort to carry on the strategy of Ida B. Wells Barnett and Martin Luther King Jr. He talked civil rights and money: "We can make them listen with our money," he declared with a list of demands in his hands. "We can stop giving it to them until they are ready to listen to us." The "Demands of the Black Community" were simple: 30-percent black employment in all places of business, desegregation of public spaces, a minimum-wage campaign for domestic workers, paved streets in black neighborhoods, the removal of the police chief and his posse, and a complete overhaul of arrest procedures. "They treat us like niggers," Perkins cried out, "but they love our nigger money!"[2]

The Montgomery, Alabama, White Citizens' Council

would have accused Perkins of inciting "violence," but this was Mississippi. A few months later, after another protest, the Rankin County police singled Perkins out, calling him "the smart nigger." On a chilly February night in 1970, inside the bowels of the Rankin County jailhouse, officers tortured Perkins to within an inch of his life. Sheriff Jonathan Edwards punched him hard in the head. Men whose duty was to protect and serve subsequently pulverized Perkins with baseball bats and nightsticks. Then, one officer shoved a fork up Perkins's nose and twisted it down his throat. They beat him again. Four hours later, they left him for dead.

Perkins lay on a steel-framed bed in the county jail; his swollen head had lumps the size of golf balls. His bed sheets were soaked through with blood. Perkins was terrified, but he had not been stopped. The black community posted bail and nursed him back to life. Within months, a more determined Perkins was traveling throughout Mississippi with a more demanding organizing schedule than before.

Before reaching this intense commitment to his cause, Perkins had experienced a profound shift. Two decades earlier in 1947, he had moved to Southern California at the urging of his family after a deputy marshal in Mississippi shot his brother Clyde, who was then turned away by local white hospitals. Clyde died. The Perkins family feared John would retaliate, so they urged him west. In California, he was heavily influenced by the Scofield Reference Bible and dispensationalist theology. Far from Mississippi, under the warmth of a Pasadena sky, Perkins found Jesus. Soon after, he became a voracious student of Jack Macarthur, famous dispensationalist radio teacher and pastor of Calvary Bible Church in Burbank. When he returned to Simpson County in 1960 with his wife, Vera Mae, and son Spencer, he did so with the conviction that evangelism was the best strategy for reform in the South.

"When he arrived back in Mississippi in 1960," writes Charles Marsh in *The Beloved Community*,

> Perkins thought of himself as a certain kind of fundamentalist Christian, a pre-millennial dispensationalist. With judgment day waiting in the wings, the dispensationalist view of history held the belief that (as historian Joel Carpenter writes) "the social application of the gospel was a waste of time." God was coming soon to transport his children to heaven in the rapture, and no one save those who had clothed themselves in holiness would be spared eternal torment.[3]

However, the Summer Project of 1964, a.k.a. "Freedom Summer," shook the foundations of Perkins's fundamentalist theology.

Freedom Summer participants, like Michael Schwerner and Andrew Goodman, came from across the United States to Mississippi to help enfranchise black southerners through voting drives, citizenship classes, and nonviolent protests. The Perkins family offered Summer Project participants a place to stay. While Perkins disapproved of the moral lives of many, he admired their courage and collaborated with their fight. By the late 1960s, Perkins found himself organizing political protests in addition to weekly Bible studies. The Project taught Perkins a lesson reminiscent of the lessons Finney and Wilberforce learned in the era of the slave trade. In Perkins's South, "New birth in Jesus meant waging war against segregation just as much as it meant putting the honky-tonks and juke joints out of business."[4] In a radical leap from his fundamentalist roots, Perkins echoed the assertions of Rauschenbusch, King, and Thurman: "Social action fleshes out the Lordship of Christ."[5]

In a recent interview, Perkins explained his concept of the good news of the Bible. He started with a basic understanding of gospel fundamentals:

> The good news is that we can have the redemption of sin because of God's love for us. We can have what we call salvation. Salvation means that we have been saved from the past—Adam's sin. We have been forgiven, then set free. We're being saved now as we live for God: he's with us, the Holy Spirit empowers us. And that he's returning, again, to set up his everlasting kingdom.

Then Perkins threw a curve ball when he spoke of the basic evangelical perception of the gospel: "We left out justice. Justice was God's motivation for redemption." According to Perkins, God took our sins away and prepared us to live a just life in society. "He redeemed us so we could live and love each other," he says.[6]

Perkins's life call and mission crystallized while he was lying on a hospital bed in Mound Bayou, Mississippi, months after the police torture. He had suffered a small heart attack and had to come back to Mound Bayou for a season of regular treatments at a local medical center. One night Perkins lay on his back staring up at the hospital room ceiling, but it wasn't the ceiling he saw. Perkins saw the frightening truth that somehow, for some reason, whites in the South were either blind or hardened to the plights of black people. Worse, whites saw no tension between their own evangelical Christian salvation and their racism—none at all. Perkins's vision went deeper. "It's the system," he wrote in his ground-breaking *Let Justice Roll Down*, "the whole structure of economic and social cages that have neatly boxed the black man in so that 'nice' people can join the oppression without getting their hands dirty—just by letting things run along."[7]

In the wake of his insights, Perkins's theological world-view transformed into a profound mix of both/and. He held on to the core values of his fundamentalist roots—personal transformation and Bible-based leadership. Yet, he integrated a deep commitment to social transformation based on justice into the core of his understanding of the gospel. That integrated worldview opened the door and made the good news of social redemption accessible to evangelical Christians throughout the United State Perkins's articulation of true discipleship in our racialized American context—the Three Rs—laid key foundations for evangelical American understanding of social justice in the late twentieth century.

THE THREE Rs

Perkins drew his Three Rs—relocation, redistribution, and reconciliation—from wisdom gained after Freedom Summer. He developed the concepts into transferable principles after his Mound Bayou experience and honed them through talks and seminars on community development throughout the early 1970s. The Three Rs guided Perkins's call for radical Christian discipleship to become the norm in the racially segregated United States if Christians were ever to deal with the issue of race and poverty in our world.

Perkins's reconciliation called evangelical Christians to *be* neighbors to each other in the same way the Samaritan proved to be the neighbor in Jesus's story (Luke 10:36–37). The Samaritan was a true neighbor because he ministered to the needs of an enemy deemed "other" with extravagant care and love. Jesus says, "Go and do likewise." Thus, Perkins called the believer to follow Jesus into the lives of "others" in order to love as the Samaritan loved. Further, Perkins's reconciliation called the church to follow the example of the ancient church in the town of Antioch: breaking down dividing walls in an interethnic community (Acts 11:19–21). Perkins's call to reconciliation is not a feel-good call, though it may seem so on the surface. There may be hugs and tears at the level of personal relationships, but eventually, the tensions of cross-ethnic relationships will surface. Different worldviews and different experiences of power and privilege in the United States and the world will come into conflict because the restoration of justice requires relocation and redistribution. Changing systems of privilege is difficult because justice requires challenging those who want to hold on to power.

Jesus, Perkins noted, offered the ultimate example of incarnational ministry as God in the flesh. Relocation is the idea of incarnation applied to ministry—ministry "in the flesh." In Jesus, the Son of God descended from heaven to be born fully human on earth. As such, Jesus was subject to every temptation and every danger known to humanity—even death on a cross. Perkins called affluent Christians to live in the image of God by removing themselves from the familiar, the comfortable, and the safe, such as malls, cafes, and sports clubs that dominate privileged life. He challenged them to choose displacement and to relocate in the unfamiliar, uncomfortable, and sometimes unsafe hotbeds of marginalization called urban ghettos or rural slums. Voluntary displacement offers affluent Christians the opportunity to follow Jesus as they experience life in the ragged shoes of their impoverished neighbors. Perkins didn't stop there. His call to relocation called upwardly mobile leaders from the community to move back and stay. In a practical sense, Perkins saw a river of human resources flowing out of impoverished communities and not into them. He placed heavy emphasis on building and maintaining the capacity of indigenous leaders within marginalized communities.

The call to relocation is counterintuitive. The natural inclination of human beings is to be self-protective. Yet Perkins sees the Christian faith as something that should motivate Jesus's followers to act with radical love on behalf of those on the margins, risking their own safety in the process. Perkins views the powers of poverty and racism in America as more substantial and powerful than any remedy that love-from-a-distance could begin to address. To face the powers of poverty and racism and the systems they rule, Christians must lock hands with the least in society to comprehend the full weight and breadth of the systemic oppression of poverty and racism. Without such close proximity to the "other," their plights remain "their" plights. "They" remain conceptual, relegated to the realms of political issues and economic theories. People called "they" remain dehumanized, even by those who claim to help from a distance, because the humanity of the poor is swallowed up in the imaginations of the affluent. They cast the impoverished in two-dimensional roles: the noble poor or the savage poor. In either case, the poor have no name, no history, no individuality, and no creative will. The poor are simply "the poor." To understand the depth of unique creative ca-

pacity that exists within the minds, souls, and strength of
oppressed human beings and to understand the complex
powers that bind them, relocation—even if only for a time—
is a mandate.

In accordance with Perkins's call to relocation, sociolo-
gists Michael Emerson and Christian Smith discovered a
phenomenon among white evangelicals who had been displaced into a network or community of color. Their worldviews were broadened. They gained the cultural tools of
structuralism and historical worldview. "It appears whites
need networks of blacks," Emerson and Smith explain, "such
as in neighborhoods, places of worship, work, and school, because this significantly reduces their interracial isolation."[8]
Further:

> Under the condition of extensive cross-race net-
> works, white evangelicals modified the use of their
> cultural tools and their racial understandings, so
> much so that their understandings began to resem-
> ble those of African-Americans. This suggests an im-
> portant possibility. If white evangelicals were less
> racially isolated, they might assess race problems dif-
> ferently and, working in unison with others, apply
> their evangelical vigor to broader-based solutions.[9]

Perkins intuited this problem and called white evangelicals to relocate into marginalized communities. Informed by
his Mound Bayou revelation, Perkin's view of poverty and
racism expanded and deepened. He came to understand
these powers as foundational forces that twist the lives of
both the oppressed and the affluent. The souls of those
who benefit from oppressive systems are distorted as the

self-preserving quests for money, power, and control cause them to dehumanize others. All humanity is in need of salvation from the oppressive powers of race and poverty. Radical counterintuitive measures are needed to address oppression in sufficient measure. Just as Mary, the mother of Jesus, released her child to live the call set before him—even death on a cross—so too, Perkins noted, the way of faith calls Christians to cling to God, not their physical well-being, for the sake of the call. Followers of Jesus are called to displace themselves for the sake of the oppressed and for the sake of the souls of those twisted by privilege. The problem of oppression is so deep and pervasive that the radical call to love others must move believers even to the point where they exercise Paul's call: "Let each of you look not to your own interests, but to the interests of others" (Philippians 2:4).

With his third R, redistribution, Perkins called for evangelical Christians to take their resources (such as talent, education, skills, networks, and funding), concentrated in affluent enclaves of society, and use them to create a more equitable world. Perkins also called for the redistribution of public resources and equity in public policy. In a 2006 interview, Perkins outlined a surprisingly simple and workable plan for U.S. reparations for slavery:

> What we would guarantee is educational opportunity. That would bring a sense of redistribution. I remember in the '70s, we talked about the idea that every [African American] child who was born will begin to get some type of a savings account starting at $4000–$5000. By the time that child was eighteen years old, they would have the basic funding needed

to pay for their college education. And that would guarantee every child a chance at a decent life.[10]

Perkins's understanding of redistribution is much more radical, much more costly, and much more Christian than sharing resources. Christians must redistribute *both* their personal resources *and* their systemic privilege. Christians must press for public policies that redistribute public resources as well.

In a more recent interview, Perkins explained the conundrum that evangelicals confront when faced with the need to apologize for slavery:

> The great redemptive story, prior to Christ's incarnation and his death on the cross, was the story where God saved the nation of Israel from Egyptian slavery. So, if ending slavery was the method that God was going to use to show his redemptive love, then you would think—just on a political level—you would think Christians would take leadership saying, "Let's repent and apologize for the enslavement of black people." But what we would call conservative evangelicals would probably oppose that, in reality.[11]

To date, only Virginia, Maryland, North Carolina, and Alabama have offered formal state apologies for slavery—all in 2007. The United States federal government has never formally apologized for the policies that authorized and enforced the use of human beings as chattel.

The Three Rs established the bedrock of Perkins's vision for evangelical discipleship in the United States. In 1971, he created the Freedom Summer Project at his Voice of Calvary Ministries (VOC) as a kind of "historical bookend"[12] to the Freedom Summer of 1964, only this time it would take an evangelical approach. An experiment in cross-ethnic community, Perkins's Project brought together white fundamentalist students from California with militant black students from the University of Michigan.

Perkins identified that summer as the "biggest failure in Voice of Calvary history."[13] The experiment failed because of the extremes in the make-up of the community and the short-term nature of the project. The white students came armed with their Scofield Bibles and expected to focus on saving souls, while the black students prepared by reading Eldridge Cleaver and black-power literature. In addition, this community of extremes had only a short-term investment in each other. They felt little need to come to any common understanding. Perkins determined that ethnic reconciliation could not be manufactured. It had to come in the context of committed community. From that point on, Perkins determined to seek repentance, forgiveness, and reconciliation primarily within the committed interracial VOC community.

Through the community of VOC, generations of students would make a pilgrimage to summer project experiences that continue to this day.[14] The main difference between these new summer projects and Freedom Summer 1971 is that, in '71, the students themselves made up the base community. On future projects, students were integrated into the already established community of VOC. The students came to observe and learn from a community investing in the Three Rs on a daily basis. Since this time summer immersion projects have become a normative part of the evangelical experience. As summer projects became normative, a new generation began to implement the Three Rs in daily life. They relocated into urban and rural slums, redistributed their resources, and engaged interethnic communities in the process of becoming reconciled.

In the late 1980s Perkins realized he should help to form a national network of these communities and organizations. In 1989 he called together a group of Christian leaders bound by the single commitment to express the love of Christ at the grassroots level in impoverished communities. An association was formed that year, and the Christian Community Development Association (CCDA) gathered for the first time in Chicago. Two hundred individuals and thirty-seven organizations became members. In 2008 the organization reported over eight thousand individual members and hundreds of organizational members. This network has served to embed the principles of the Three Rs in the evangelical paradigm of what it means to do justice, love mercy, and walk humbly with God. In addition, CCDA's annual conference serves as an effective instrument to pass these foundations to younger generations.

LEGACY

Though John M. Perkins is a relatively inconspicuous figure outside evangelical circles, he is crucial in U.S. evangelical history in the second half of the twentieth century. Two seemingly disparate worlds came together with equal force in this one man—Scofield's fundamentalist world and the world of Rauschenbusch's social gospel. Perkins's personal struggle to reconcile the two in himself broke down a barrier that divided the evangelical universe. Two theological camps, divorced at the turn of the twentieth century, were given a chance at reconciliation. Perkins offered a both/and theology, one that stayed true to the gospel's power and purpose to transform individuals while grasping again the forgotten revolutionary truth that God's good news *also* trumpets Jesus's commitment to transform the social order of society, bringing individuals and social-political systems into right relationship with each other.

Though Martin Luther King Jr. drew from the well of black evangelical Christology in his later years, his faith was not nurtured in the context of the white evangelical church. As a result, his message was silenced or demonized in white evangelical circles. Thus, it took Perkins, whose faith was born in the white evangelical context, to reach white evangelicals. The authority Perkins gave to the scriptures, his relentless belief in personal transformation, and his spiritual heritage as one reared in the fundamentalist church all gave Perkins a unique capacity to translate "liberal" values into scripture-based principles that evangelicals could hear and understand. Likewise, his experiences as a black man gave him clear understanding of the racial and economic idolatry embedded in the souls of the white southerners he encountered. His experiences were also grounded in the beloved community he encountered in the Freedom Summer Project of 1964. Since the 1960s Perkin's Three Rs, interethnic community-based work embodied in Voice of Calvary, short-term summer immersion projects, and the Christian Community Development Association have worked together to pave the road for generations of evangelicals to wed Jesus and justice in their worldviews and their life's work.

PROPHETS WITH OLD AND NEW
CULTURAL TOOL KITS

Perkins, a black man, was born again and mentored in a white fundamentalist network. As a result, he adopted what Michael Emerson and Christian Smith call "white evangelical cultural tools" to interpret the world. Given the Emerson and Smith theory, Perkins's story raises an intriguing question: is it possible for African Americans to adopt typically white cultural tools when immersed in a white context? And if so, is it possible for them to regain the cultural tools they laid down when they were "born again" in the white context?

Perkins's life offers a relevant case study. As a result of his immersion in white fundamentalist community networks, Perkins believed all that was needed to eliminate racism in the South was for individuals to get saved—what we might call an antistructural, freewill individualist, relational worldview. The natural result would be that things would get better. This worldview ignores structural or systemic oppression and fails to see connections between racism and forces greater than the individual and personal sin. When Perkins reimmersed himself in an African American community, he realized those cultural tools could not make sense of the depth and breadth of the evil he encountered in Mississippi. Perkins experienced a radical and painful worldview shift that white evangelicals would experience upon relocating and entering Voice of Calvary Ministries for the first time. Perkins intuitively crafted what Emerson and Smith suggest is the ideal structure for white evangelicals to undergo their own worldview shift.

Quantifying Perkins's influence is difficult. His Three Rs, the summer project model he borrowed from the civil rights movement and transplanted into the evangelical world, and the impact of the CCDA network have worked synergistically, with each strengthening the impact of the other. Together, they laid the foundations for the current awakening among younger U.S. evangelicals, who increasingly accept without question that racial justice is a central call of the gospel.

John M. Perkins continues to be a leader whose thinking and methodology has laid vital foundations for the current shift occurring within evangelical America. When he preached on the courthouse steps in 1970, he was more than a prophet in the wilderness. He was not and is not alone. Like Isaiah, Micah, Hosea, and Amos—all of whom spoke consistent words of rebuke, correction, and hope to Israel—Perkins and his contemporaries called the evangelical church back to itself, to its true roots in the gospel of Jesus Christ. Perkins opened a door in the evangelical universe, and a small but mighty community of prophets stepped through the door. They were black and white. And they were committed to one thing: reconciling a divided evangelical church for the sake of justice for all and for the sake of God's glory.

Tom Skinner was the first African American speaker to give a keynote speech at InterVarsity Christian Fellowship's Urbana mission convention. A converted gang leader from Harlem, Skinner's 1970 Urbana speech, officially called "The U.S. Racial Crisis and World Evangelism" but commonly called "The Liberator Has Come," marked the turning point in the organization's perceptions of the gospel. Skinner led eleven thousand college students, theologians, and missionaries through a comprehensive history of race relations on U.S. soil and the African American quest for liberation. He preached a message that married racial justice and economic justice with the coming of the kingdom of God. On that night, Skinner did what no speaker had done before at an Urbana convention. He punched a hole in the white evangelical bubble and proclaimed the gospel from the bottom of society.

Skinner scolded the Protestant church for its compliance with the deadly divorce of social justice from personal transformation. He looked at both the Rauschenbusch camp and the Scofield camp and said, "Both positions were wrong." He explained:

> Both were extremes. Both compartmentalized me. One said, "Just give him a passport out of hell to heaven, get him saved, give him eternal life and never mind about his oppression. Never mind about the fact that he has to live with rats and roaches. Never mind that he's a fourth-class citizen. Never mind that he will be shot on sight. Never mind that there are places that he can't go." On the other hand the liberal compartmentalized me because he wanted only to feed my belly. He did not see me as a total spiritual being.[15]

Skinner shined a glaring light on evangelicals' silent approval of racial segregation and lynching throughout the post-Reconstruction era. At the same time, he affirmed the need for personal liberation from spiritual oppression.

> There is no possible way you can talk about preaching the gospel if you do not want to deal with the is-

sues that bind people. If your gospel is an "either-or" gospel, I must reject it. Any gospel that does not talk about delivering to man a personal Savior who will free him from the personal bondage of sin and grant him eternal life and does not at the same time speak to the issue of enslavement, the issue of injustice, the issue of inequality—any gospel that does not want to go where people are hungry and poverty-stricken and set them free in the name of Jesus Christ is not the gospel.[16]

He called for Americans to divest from the idolatry of the "God and country" merger that stops the ears of evangelicals, making it impossible to critique the actions of their own country. "God will not be without a witness," he said. "Jesus Christ pulled off one of the greatest political coups of all time: He got up out of the grave. . . . The Bible now calls him the second man, the new man, the leader of a new creation. A Christ who has overthrown the existing order and established a new order that is not built on man." He continued, "Proclaim liberation to the captives, preach sight to the blind, set at liberty them that are bruised, go into the world and tell men that are bound mentally, spiritually and physically, 'The liberator has come.' " Skinner announced this to an audience that rose to its feet in thunderous applause, harbingers of a 1970s evangelical Jesus movement.

That Jesus movement recruited a new generation from within white evangelical America. Largely influenced by Anabaptist pacifism, Wesleyan holiness, the Catholic Worker movement, the traditional black church, and the civil rights movement, leaders like Jim Wallis, Tony Campolo, and Ron Sider spoke to white evangelical America from the margins.

They echoed the calls of Skinner and Perkins. These late-twentieth-century white prophets are textbook case studies in Emerson and Smith's theory of religion and racism in the United States. Each of them experienced prolonged immersion in African American communities. Their experiences shifted their worldview, and they incorporated a nuanced understanding of systemic injustice.

Jim Wallis and a band of countercultural graduates of Trinity Divinity School in Illinois committed to the Three Rs. They moved to a disenfranchised African American neighborhood in Washington, D.C., where they lived out a Christian model of community, sharing things in common. Everyone was paid the same salary, regardless of their position. Everyone contributed to a community fund that paid for rent, utilities, and groceries. Their prophetic Christian community also sought to address issues of policy affecting the poor and oppressed. Their magazine, the *Post-American*, would become *Sojourners*, while their community evolved into a national movement, also called Sojourners. The movement networks individuals, churches, and organizations committed to social justice. In a break from the focus on personal and interpersonal transformation typical of white evangelical calls for justice, Wallis's 1992 treatise *A Call to Conversion* challenged evangelical Christians to consider the social *and political* implications of personal faith.

Wallis and the Sojourners movement have consistently pressed evangelical Americans to return to their nineteenth-century abolitionist roots. They fight for the abolition of poverty and urge evangelicals to engage in the political arena. When asked in a recent interview why Sojourners has focused on political engagement as opposed to traditional Christian community development, Wallis answered:

You know, William Booth and Katherine Booth, founders of the Salvation Army, said it well when they began. They said, "You can't keep picking people up at the bottom of the mountain and not send somebody climbing the hill to see what's pushing people over the edge." You've got to talk about causes and not just symptoms and outcomes.[17]

Thus, Sojourners focuses on the systemic causes of poverty and shines light on the public policies that have potential to oppress or bless impoverished communities across the country.

The political dominance of the Religious Right has led the media to refer to Wallis as representing "the Religious Left." Wallis opposes this categorization:

I think Left and Right are political categories and not religious ones. Religion doesn't fit those categories of Left and Right. They're not our categories. So, I often say, "Don't go Left. Don't go Right. Go deeper." We're not a Religious Left to counter a Religious Right, but rather a moral center, often challenging the selective moralities of both the Right and the Left.[18]

In living out of the moral center, Wallis tries to talk to people across the political spectrum, Republican or Democrat. At Sojourners/Call to Renewal conferences Sam Brownback is as likely to speak as Hillary Clinton and Barack Obama. The goal is not party alignment but alignment with the poor. As a result, Wallis partners with those on both sides of the aisle who work for the poor. Sojourners gained prominence during the 2004 and 2006 election campaigns because the message that Wallis had preached since the beginning finally found a platform in Democratic circles. In the wake of the Bush administration's failed foreign policies and the mounting scandals surrounding members of the Religious Right, the nation was hungry for moral leadership that prioritized poverty and peace. Spotlights and TV cameras shined on Wallis, who was asked for his perspective at every turn. Wallis understands doing justice, however, as first and foremost an act of worship. At his conferences he calls everyone in attendance to worship as they do justice together.

Tony Campolo has a publication list a mile long, and it is as diverse as the city he calls home, Philadelphia. His sermons touch on subjects from economic and racial justice to politics and sexual purity. But it was his speech "It's Friday, but Sunday's Coming!"—a call to personal and social transformation—that launched one of the most influential evangelical preachers of the late twentieth century.

When African Americans streamed into northern cities from the 1920s to the 1950s, white families responded by leaving the cities en masse. They searched for whiter pastures. Philadelphia was no different. Campolo was born there in 1935—the year Babe Ruth hit his last home run, the year the Dust Bowl swept the nation, the year Nazi Germany adopted a new national flag with a swastika on its face, and the year the U.S. Social Security Act was passed and ensured financial protection for senior citizens. Campolo's early experiences shaped a life focused on justice. The Campolo family's West Philadelphia neighborhood experienced white flight throughout the 1930s and '40s. Campolo's childhood church closed when white parishioners decided to flee the inner city. A few either could not or would not leave. Campolo's Sicilian father would not. Instead, he found the closest available church—a black Baptist church—and his family switched membership. Campolo has been a member there ever since.

Often inaccurately grouped with Wallis under the category "Religious Left," or called "liberal" by conservative evangelicals, Campolo has sloughed off these monikers in favor of the more accurate "Red-Letter Christian." The term was first used by a secular Jewish disc jockey in Nashville, Tennessee. His term refers to older styles of printing Bibles, which used red to highlight words attributed to Jesus. The disc jockey named Christians who took social justice issues seriously "red letter" because so much of what Jesus said was about justice. It stuck.

> We began to use the phrase "Red-Letter Christians," referring to the red letters in the New Testament, the words of Jesus. In some corners the minute you say "evangelical" red flags go up and they assume you're anti-gay, you're opposed to women in church leadership roles, you are some kind of anti-environmentalist, you are pro-war, and you're pro-guns. And we're saying, "Hey! That's not who we are." [19]

Campolo is a white man raised in a predominately African American community. He endured racism with friends and neighbors on a daily basis. He sat in church and heard sermons about overcoming and being patient about carrying the weight of oppression because "Sunday's a comin'!" Campolo's upbringing made it virtually impossible to ignore interpersonal and systemic racism. Consequently, from the beginning of his career, his messages have called evangelicals to repent of interpersonal and systemic racism and economic injustice.

Campolo does not consider himself a prophet, but he is. He speaks to conservative evangelicals hundreds of times per year. He was the target of heresy charges brought by a group of fundamentalist pastors in 1985. Though found innocent by a panel of evangelical leaders led by J.I. Packer, author of *Knowing God* and *Concise Theology: A Guide to Historic Christian Beliefs*, Campolo continues to be labeled "liberal" among many conservative evangelicals. He is, however, an evangelical in the classic nineteenth-century sense of the word. Like the ancestors, Campolo's good news is both personal and social, and in all things, it is transformative. It proclaims that God seeks to transform individuals, even as God transforms systems and societies.

Ron Sider was born in 1939 into a Brethren in Christ preacher's family and grew up on a farm in Stevensville, Ontario, just two miles north of the Niagara River. He could see Buffalo, New York, on the other side. His family's religious foundations were built on a synthesis of strong Anabaptist and Mennonite values, which set the course for Sider's life, one dedicated to the Anabaptist commitment to economic justice and the Mennonite commitment to pacifism and peacemaking. The Wesleyan value of personal holiness was also adopted by Sider's family.[20] Renowned for his 1977 classic *Rich Christians in an Age of Hunger,* Sider is well known in the evangelical church for his call for Christians to be fiscally generous in an age of global poverty.

It is rare for Sider's name to be linked to the issue of American race relations. However, this go-to prophet for fiscal stewardship was catalyzed to action by racial injustice.

He joined his first protest march at Waterloo Lutheran College in 1960 against apartheid. When blacks in South Africa organized to demonstrate against the new Pass Law System, police gunned them down. Sixty died. One hundred seventy-eight were wounded. The Sharpsville Massacre ignited protests around the world. Sider counts that protest at Waterloo among the key experiences that ignited his deep commitment to justice. There were others.

Sider joined InterVarsity while at Yale University, which he attended from 1962–68. He rented a room from an African American family and was with them the night Dr. Martin Luther King Jr. was assassinated. They sat together. They talked. With awe, Sider recalls two things about that night: the simmering anger of the couple's twenty-five-year-old son and his incredible "openness to talk to a white kid who wanted to listen and learn."[21] However, Sider counts his move to North Philadelphia as the point of no return in his understanding of racial and economic injustice. His denominational school, Messiah College in rural Pennsylvania, was setting up an extension campus at Temple University in the middle of Philadelphia. He and his wife, Arbutus, moved there with their children when Sider accepted an invitation to teach at the new extension campus. They enrolled their children in the public schools and lived as one of few white families in the neighborhood from 1968 to 1975. After graduate school the Siders moved to Germantown, a mixed-income neighborhood that changed from 65 percent to 90 percent African American during the twenty-three years they lived there.

On the first page of the preface to his 1999 groundbreaking book *Just Generosity: A New Vision for Overcom-*

ing Poverty in America, Sider lists the experiences that rocked his soul and ignited his heart and mind on behalf of the poor:

> My wife, Arbutus, and I have joined our neighbors to shut down a drug house a few doors up the street. We have added locks and helped organize our block to help residents feel more secure. We have watched moms and dads do battle with their drug addiction for the sake of their kids. We have held those children in their pain as mom or dad let them down. We have cheered on dramatic transformation rooted in spiritual conversion, and we have watched helpless while others lost the struggle. We have listened with sadness and resentment as members of our church looked in vain for a job to help them care for their family. We have muttered in anger as cancer suddenly overwhelmed a hardworking and temporarily jobless, and therefore uninsured, fellow elder in our church with $100,000 in medical bills that he knew he could never pay.[22]

He dedicated the book to "friends and neighbors in North Philly and Germantown who have taught me so much."[23]

Sider believes unequivocally that Christians could help to end poverty if they wanted to. This has been his message for thirty years. The scandal is that those who claim to follow Christ do not want to—not nearly enough. People continue to live and die on the rack of poverty in the richest nation on earth, while Christians justify their inaction using statistics taken out of context, racist assumptions about the character of many living under the burden of poverty, and false strategic compartmentalizations.

In *Just Generosity*, Sider debunks three influential theories of poverty reduction. He deems as unwarranted Michael Harrington's socialist confidence in the unique power of the federal government to end poverty in the United States. Sider believes Charles Murray's conservative theory, which espouses the need to stop all government aid to the poor to force them to pull themselves up by their own bootstraps, abandons too many. Finally, he views Marvin Olasky's compassionate conservative theory, which touts the matchless power of charitable, faith-based programs to reduce poverty, as partially true, but tragically flawed. Sider contends that the federal government, individual effort, and the best charitable Christian programs *cannot* solve the problem of poverty on their own. Rather, it is only possible to end poverty if these strategies work together in concert. *Just Generosity* outlines a comprehensive, interrelated strategy to bring poverty in the United States to an end.

Like Wallis and Campolo, Sider has been changed to the core through the experience of prolonged immersion in a network of African American relationships. Sider explains: "Many, many of the people I know who care deeply about racial and economic justice have had their own experiential encounter with hurting people. I'm sure that's a crucial piece of it." These displaced white evangelicals illustrate what Emerson and Smith discovered about what it takes to grasp the systemic dimensions of oppression.

CONCLUSION

Perkins, Skinner, Wallis, Campolo, and Sider offer evangelical America a picture of what is possible when evangelicals cross racial networks and modify their cultural tool kits. These prophets are in the trenches together working for both a personal *and* a social gospel. Wallis, Campolo, Sider, and Perkins were arrested together in 2006 when they engaged in peaceful protest calling on Congress to regard the national budget as a moral document that reveals what and who this country values. I believe Skinner would have been there too, if he had still been alive. These prophets worked together, preached together, learned from each other, and spoke the same message of the kingdom of God to an unjust world.

The drama of the evangelical church over almost two centuries is clear: the evangelical church has shined brightest when confronting two of the most fundamental problems in U.S. society: race and poverty. These were the beachhead issues addressed by the abolitionist movement, the civil rights movement, and the twentieth-century great awakening led by John Perkins, Tom Skinner, Jim Wallis, Ron Sider and Tony Campolo. They called the church back to itself and pressed for engagement in social issues with a deep faith worthy of the glory of God.

3

Jilted and Framed

I remember the devotion of your youth, your love as a bride, how you followed me in the wilderness, in a land not sown. . . . What wrong did your ancestors find in me that they went far from me, and went after worthless things, and became worthless things themselves? . . . For my people have committed two evils: they have forsaken me, the fountain of living water, and dug out cisterns for themselves, cracked cisterns that can hold no water.

—Jeremiah 2:2,5,13

"I write as a jilted lover," Randall Balmer confesses in the first line of his 2006 memoir, *Thy Kingdom Come: An Evangelical's Lament.* He continues: "The evangelical faith that nurtured me as a child and sustains me as an adult has been hijacked by right-wing zealots who have distorted the gospel of Jesus Christ, defaulted on the noble legacy of nineteenth-century evangelical activism, and failed to appreciate the genius of the First Amendment."[1] Balmer, professor of American religious history at Barnard College, was an eyewitness to evangelical adultery. The affair began in 1970.

In the same year John Perkins was tortured in a Mississippi jail, parents of black children in Mississippi filed a class-action suit, *Green v. Connally*, against private schools that whites set up as "segregation academies" in response to the U.S. Supreme Court's 1954 decision in *Brown v. Board of Education of Topeka*. Schools throughout Mississippi discriminated against applicants based on race, yet kept their tax-exempt status. *Green v. Connally* was decided in 1971 in favor of the parents. The court upheld a 1967 IRS ruling that declared it unlawful for schools that practice racial discrimination to receive federal tax-exempt status.[2] This district court ruling only affected segregated schools in Mississippi. Nevertheless, the IRS saw this ruling as validation of its longstanding "national policy to discourage racial discrimination in education." The IRS issued a ruling that it would no longer grant tax-exempt status to schools practicing racial discrimination.[3]

Bob Jones University, established in 1927 at the height of the fundamentalist revolt, is a nondenominational fundamentalist institution located in Greenville, South Carolina. The university's "Fast Facts" Web page currently boasts it is "the world's largest fundamental Christian School." True to its founder's segregationist worldview, the university prohibited the admission of African Americans. The IRS informed Bob Jones University in 1970 that its tax-exempt status would be revoked, but the school maintained that it was entitled to tax exemption as a religious institution. Nonetheless, it began accepting applications for admission from African Americans, if they were married within their own race. It continued to deny admission to unmarried and interracially married African Americans.[4]

In 1975, the Fourth Circuit Court of Appeals outlawed the practice of racial discrimination by all private schools. The university was notified on April 16, 1975, that its tax-exempt status would be revoked. On January 19, 1976, it was made official: the IRS revoked the university's tax-exempt status. Bob Jones was compelled to allow admission to unmarried African American applicants, but enforced a policy against interracial dating that read:

> There is to be no interracial dating.
> 1. Students who are partners in an interracial marriage will be expelled.
> 2. Students who are members of or affiliated with any group or organization which holds as one of its goals or advocates interracial marriage will be expelled.
> 3. Students who date outside of their own race will be expelled.
> 4. Students who espouse, promote, or encourage others to violate the University's dating rules and regulations will be expelled.[5]

In 1976, the university filed tax returns for the period from December 1, 1970, to December 31, 1975, accompanied by a payment of $21 in taxes for one employee for the calendar year 1975. The IRS countered with a letter informing the school that it owed $489,675.59 in taxes, plus interest. The university filed a petition to reinstate its tax-exempt status based on the freedom of religion clause of the First Amendment. That petition would be argued in the courts for the next seven years.

This is where a sad, revealing story turns tragic.

JILTED

Randall Balmer was invited to an exclusive Religious Right conference in Washington in 1990. At this conference, Balmer sat in a room with the likes of:

> Ralph Reed, then leader of the Christian Coalition; Carl F.H. Henry, an evangelical theologian; Tom Minnery of Focus on the Family; Donald Wildmon, head of the American Family Association; Richard Land of the Southern Baptist Convention; and Edward G. Dobson, pastor of an evangelical church in Grand Rapids, Michigan, and formerly one of Jerry Falwell's acolytes at Moral Majority. Paul Weyrich, a longtime conservative activist, head of what is now called the Free Congress Foundation, and one of the architects of the Religious Right in the late 1970s, was also there.[6]

In the course of one session, Balmer remembers, someone tried to make a point by emphasizing the origins of their movement—*Roe v. Wade*. Weyrich vehemently opposed that marker of the movement's genesis. "Weyrich insisted," says Balmer, "what got us going as a political movement was the attempt on the part of the Internal Revenue Service (IRS) to rescind the tax-exempt status of Bob Jones University because of its racially discriminatory policies."[7]

Weyrich had campaigned for Barry Goldwater and had been working ever since "to energize evangelical voters over school prayer, abortion, or the proposed equal rights amendment to the Constitution."[8] He had failed. Then came *Green v. Connally* and Bob Jones University's revoked tax-exempt status, and, finally, Jimmy Carter was elected president. A Democrat and devout Southern Baptist, Jimmy Carter was elected largely because a loose network of evangelical leaders rallied support for his campaign. In response to his election, *Time* declared that 1976 was the Year of the Evangelical. Some of those evangelical leaders supported Carter in the hopes that they could exert influence once he took office. But Carter was a true-blue Baptist. He believed in the First Amendment disestablishment of religion. Thus, disillusioned leaders like Weyrich allied against him. Though the IRS decision to revoke Bob Jones University's tax-exempt status predated Carter's presidency, Weyrich and other Religious Right leaders convinced the evangelical public that Carter was the one responsible for the IRS revoking the university's status. Balmer recounts Weyrich's revelry in an early 1990s interview in which Weyrich explained how the movement galvanized support for antiabortionism and other far-right issues: " 'I was trying to get those people interested in those issues and utterly failed. What changed their mind was Jimmy Carter's intervention against the Christian schools, trying to deny them tax-exempt status on the basis of de facto segregation.' "[9]

Jimmy Carter lost his bid for a second presidential term. Several factors converged in 1979, not the least of which was the work of Paul Weyrich, Jerry Falwell, and Pat Robertson, who partnered to align evangelical support behind Ronald Reagan and the Republican Party. When Reagan took office, he gave them his ear. In fact, one of his early actions in office was to declare support for Bob Jones University and its right to tax-exempt status despite its racist policies. Nonetheless, the Supreme Court issued its verdict in 1983, siding against

Bob Jones University, whose tax-exempt status was finally and·fully revoked. That was a blow, but a small one compared to the benefits of the case for the far Right and Republican Party, for *Green v. Connally* and *Bob Jones University v. The United States* roused the Religious Right. The Reagan years solidified Religious Right support for his presidency, and evangelicals also aligned overwhelmingly with the Republican Party.

The implications of this political history are severe. The abortion myth is still very much alive and well within the evangelical world. The Religious Right currently markets itself as the new abolitionist movement. It frames its antiabortion work in a way that creates the illusion of a purpose that parallels the evangelical abolitionists of the nineteenth century. The nineteenth-century evangelicals, however, worked to *free* African Americans from bondage. The Religious Right, on the other hand, galvanized to *perpetuate* racial discrimination against African Americans, under the guise of a "pro-life" banner. Worse, to this day, Bob Jones University shows no remorse for its racist policies. The university's official Web page currently sports a picture of a smiling Reagan walking side by side with university president Dr. Bob Jones III. The text under the picture reads: "After a twelve-year legal battle with the IRS, the Supreme Court removed Bob Jones University's tax-exempt status. What some thought was certain to be a deathblow only increased the school's growth and effectiveness for the cause of Christ." [10] That's all. They fail to mention their history of racial discrimination. They express no regret on behalf of the university for its historic segregationist policies and no repentance for its discriminatory history. Instead, they insist they have grown in the face of government persecution.

FRAMED

The skulduggery did not stop there. The Religious Right's lustful pursuit of political power in the early 1980s eventually led to a complex web of deceptive media messaging. The web was spun to mobilize evangelical Christians around political platform issues like abortion, war, anti-immigration, and indiscriminate support for the state of Israel. They stirred righteous indignation in their followers based on twisted conceptions of "justice" and ignited one of the most effective collective action campaigns of the twentieth century using a right-wing "values" frame.[11]

According to William A. Gamson's *Talking Politics*, in order to successfully mobilize people for action, collective action movements always offer one or more *collective action frames* that reinforce certain values. Basic frames are simply ways to organize ideas around those values.[12] They include symbols, metaphors, visual images, and language. Pastors use them. Politicians use them. Marketers use them. In fact, we all use them to some degree. Gamson uses the example of affirmative action. The affirmative action concept is "informed and shaped by an implicit organizing idea or *frame*. . . . It assumes that racial discrimination is not a remnant of the past but a continuing presence, albeit in subtle form. It rests on the abstract and difficult idea of institutional racism."[13]

Collective action frames are, according to Gamson, dynamic sets of beliefs and meanings that compel individuals to take action together against a clear adversary to bring justice to bear in a specific situation. Collective action frames have three necessary components: (1) an issue of injustice that gives rise to moral indignation (i.e., *injustice frames*); (2) a belief in the ability of collective agency to make a difference (i.e., *presentation of effective models for action*); and (3) identification of the self (*we*) in relationship to an adversarial human agent (*them*) (i.e., *adversarial frames*).[14]

The Religious Right uses a "new abolitionist" injustice frame to attach nobility and honor to several fronts in the movement's political platforms, while at the same time opening a floodgate of righteous indignation against adversaries of its "righteous" causes. Current "new abolitionist" fronts of the Religious Right include the antiabortion battle and the war in Iraq.

In a March 2006 *Citizen* article, "Sad but Noble," William J. Stuntz provided a stark example of the Religious Right's use of the injustice frame on the "new abolitionist."[15] *Citizen* is a monthly publication of Focus on the Family. Stuntz, a Harvard law professor specializing in criminal law, sets up his injustice frame by likening George W. Bush and the Iraq war to Abraham Lincoln and the Civil War, arguing that both presidents fought for democracy and freedom from tyranny. This frame, in turn, invokes righteous indignation toward any who would dare oppose the Iraq war. Those who oppose it become adversaries. Stuntz adds weight to his collective action frame by adding a second, clearer adversary, "one of the many Mohammed Attas that Middle Eastern autocracies have bred over the last generation."[16] Stuntz warns if the United States gives up too soon, one of those Mohammed Attas could strike the United States, "and we may face a mushroom cloud over Manhattan."[17] While this article did not offer a concrete way for readers to take collective action, it was published in an issue that promoted an upcoming Focus on the Family training conference called the Truth Project. Attendees were promised training that would equip them to lead local small groups across the country, which would promote Focus on the Family's "Christian worldview." *World*, a publication designed to resemble *Newsweek* and *Time*, reported a 2006 readership of 130,000.[18] It offers a deeper example of the practice of collective action framing in a Christian media source just right of center on the political spectrum. Editor-in-chief Marvin Olasky's February 25, 2006, cover story, "Nuke Nightmare," placed *World* in similar company with Stuntz and *Citizen*. The article is flanked by a picture of the New York City skyline doctored with a fiery mushroom cloud in the background just beyond the Empire State Building.[19] This visual image created an immediate injustice frame. It evoked an emotional response of righteous indignation and fear that anyone could even think to bomb the United States. Though *World* prides itself on professional standards of reporting news and not propaganda, "Nuke Nightmare" cut corners in reporting and ultimately functioned as a case for alignment with the Bush administration.

"Nuke Nightmare" opened with a September 12, 2001, quote from Peggy Noonan, a former Reagan speechwriter and a columnist for the *Wall Street Journal*: "for some reason, and we don't even know what it was, the terrorists didn't use a small nuclear weapon floated into New York on a barge in the East River."[20] Olasky says Noonan

suspected that "the next time the bad guys hit" it will be nuclear, but "for now we have been spared. And now chastened and shaken, we are given another chance, maybe the last chance, to commit ourselves seriously and at some cost to protecting our country."[21]

But Olasky had changed the quote, as much as he did the picture of the New York City skyline. Reflecting on the events of September 11, 2001, Noonan originally said:

> We are lucky that this didn't turn nuclear, chemical or biological. It could have, and *I thought the next time the bad guys hit it would have* [emphasis added]. *Instead they used* [emphasis added] more "conventional" weapons, fuel-heavy airliners and suicide bombers. And so the number of dead will be in the thousands or tens of thousands and not millions or tens of millions.
>
> *We have been spared* [emphasis added]. And now, chastened and shaken, we are given another chance, maybe the last chance, to commit ourselves seriously and at some cost to protecting our country.[22]

The difference in intended meaning between Noonan's original quote and Olasky's reprint is clear. While Noonan spoke as an observer of the events of September 11, 2001, with reference to past beliefs regarding terrorist strategies on U.S. soil, Olasky's alteration of her quote made it appear as if Noonan intended to predict the future. Olasky wrote, "She suspected that 'the next time the bad guys hit' it *will* [emphasis added] be nuclear."[23] Olasky changed the verb "would" to "will." He didn't include the word "will" inside the quotation marks. Rather, he changed the meaning by changing the verb from past participle to future tense. In addition, he added words to her quote *within* quotation marks. Noonan's original quote said, "We have been spared." In this statement, Noonan seemed to give a grateful sigh of relief.

Yet Olasky wrote, "but *for now* [emphasis added] we have been spared." The addition of "for now" added an ominous, threatening tone, thus altering the meaning of the quote.

In the end, Olasky's use of language created a frame that evoked a response of indignation and fear and justified the Bush administration's policies regarding the war on terror and the Right's support of those policies.

In like fashion, the Religious Right used "the abortion myth," as Randall Balmer refers to it, to craft the original "new abolitionist" frame. Balmer explains:

> Simply put, the abortion myth is this: Leaders of the Right would have us believe that their movement began in direct response to the U.S. Supreme Court's 1973 *Roe v. Wade* decision. Politically conservative evangelical leaders were so morally outraged by the ruling that they instantly shed their apolitical stupor in order to mobilize politically in defense of the sanctity of life. Most of these leaders did so reluctantly and at great personal sacrifice, risking the obloquy of their congregants and the contempt of liberals and "secular humanists," who were trying their best to ruin America. But these selfless, courageous leaders of the Religious Right, inspired by the opponents of slavery in the nineteenth century, trudged dutifully into battle in order to defend those innocent unborn children, newly endangered by the Supreme Court's misguided Roe decision.[24]

Regardless of one's position in the abortion debates, the roots of the movement are not as the Right frames them. By equating the antiabortion struggle with the abolitionist struggle, the Right has created a potent injustice frame. The frame is applied to the millions of unborn babies being killed by calloused mothers each year, while society stands by and stubbornly approves. It is very compelling. The emotionally manipulative messaging evokes a sense of righteous indignation and calls for action. The problem, though, is that only one course of action is offered to remedy the situation— appoint conservative Republican presidents who will appoint conservative Supreme Court judges who will overturn *Roe v. Wade.*

There are better ways to decrease the occurrence of abortions and preserve life inside and outside of the womb. According to the Guttmacher Institute's January 2008 report on abortion trends, poor and low-income women account for more than half of all abortions in the United States. While whites account for greater numbers of abortions than other ethnic groups, the rates of abortion among blacks and Latinos far exceed the rates among whites. Abortion is fundamentally an issue of economic justice. The Guttmacher report clearly shows abortion rates drop dramatically when the government has effective systems in place to provide financial assistance to the poor. That assistance helps impoverished people to choose life. The role of poverty was demonstrated by the fact that, under the Reagan administration, abortion rates held steady or increased. In fact, abortion rates reached their highest rates ever under Reagan, who drastically cut services for the poor. The Clinton administration, which increased services for the poor, saw the sharpest drop in the abortion rate since *Roe v. Wade.* Under the current Bush administration, which has cut services to the poor, the abortion rate has mostly held steady. It is, then, a reasonable argument that to decrease the occurrence of abortions in the United States the most effective strategy is to elect officials who will craft policies and systems that actively protect and provide for the needs of the poor, the marginalized, and the vulnerable among us.[25]

The Religious Right has convinced evangelicals that to be pro-life, they must vote Republican. The truth is, the most effective way to preserve the lives of unborn babies is to align with the poor and vote for candidates who align with the poor. Unfortunately, the country is beginning to taste the fruit of the strategy the Religious Right has employed—to create a conservative Supreme Court—in areas beyond abortion politics.

The fruit of the Religious Right's obsessive focus on overturning *Roe v. Wade* is the appointment of judges who would also overturn *Brown v. Board of Education of Topeka.* In 2007, the current Court heard the case of *Parents Involved in Community Schools v. Seattle School District No. 1 Et Al.* The Court sought to determine whether intentional practices to racially integrate public schools were constitutional. Both sides argued their cases using the *Brown v. Topeka* ruling. The Court ruled against intentional practices to racially integrate public schools. Justice Breyer objected to the ruling, partially on the grounds that it would encourage de facto segregation—thus nullifying the effect of the landmark *Brown v. Topeka* case. Justice Roberts referenced Justice Breyer's objection in his summary of the Court's opinion. Roberts said de facto segregation is constitutional and, by implication, acceptable.[26]

I was part of a panel discussion at a Yale Divinity School conference entitled "Voices and Votes" in November 2007. I sat with Jim Wallis on my left and Richard Land on my right. Randall Balmer and Marvin Olasky were also on the panel, along with a number of other activists, historians, and journalists. At one point, Balmer said, "I want to see the church take responsibility for the welfare of the public the way it did in the 1900s. The reason we have so many hospitals today named Saint this and United Methodist that and Presbyterian this is because the church saw it as its responsibility to care for the least in society." At that, Olasky objected. He cited an article that *World* had just run. It highlighted a church that chose not to do a church-building project and chose instead to use its funds to build an orphanage in Africa. Richard Land could see I was agitated, so he handed me the microphone. After some back and forth, I said, "I'm glad you mentioned that churches are using their money to build orphanages in Africa. That's a good thing and it is happening. But when you press for the election of conservative presidents who will appoint conservative judges to the Supreme Court, and those judges overturn affirmative action initiatives, you are not helping my people." I was greeted with silence.

Afterward, a Divinity School student approached me and said he really liked what I said—most of it. "And I know it's true," he said, "that the same judges who would overturn *Roe v. Wade* are the ones who would overturn affirmative action." Then he gently nodded his head, pressed his lips together, then shook his head. "But I guess I still think it's worth it," he said.

Evangelicals have been *framed*.

In contrast to such fabricated framing, the prophets John Perkins, Tony Campolo, Jim Wallis, Tom Skinner, and Ron Sider called Christians to reclaim a holistic gospel. Meanwhile, the Religious Right was simultaneously galvanized by racial discrimination, fear, and war. The prophets called for racial justice grounded in the commands of scripture to "Love your neighbor as yourself." Meanwhile, Bob Jones University was fighting to keep African Americans out of its classrooms. The prophets looked at the Vietnam War and called for the withdrawal of troops. They said the war was unjust at its genesis and was wrecking havoc on communities of color. In contrast, the media engines of the current Religious Right did little but bolster and doctor the credibility of a similar failed war by consistently comparing the Iraq war to the Civil War and doctoring reality to press a political agenda. The prophets cried out for the lives of the poor, the marginalized, and the vulnerable to be protected from conception to death. In contrast, the framing practices of the Religious Right have called evangelicals to vote according to slogans, not facts, and to value unborn life *more than* the lives of the already born, especially those alive who are among the least in society.

It is deeply telling that the action that galvanized the Religious Right was one rooted in racial discrimination. Their agenda was holding power—power at the expense of the gospel itself. And worse, the Religious Right co-opted the moniker "evangelical" altogether and linked their polarizing politics to evangelical faith.

In my interviews with sixty-seven of the top evangelical leaders and emerging voices across North America, most voiced feelings similar to those of Randall Balmer. They felt jilted. They felt framed. Some still call themselves evangelicals, defying the Right to steal their heritage completely. Some call themselves postevangelicals. Others call themselves Jesus followers or followers of the Jesus way. I like that one.

Balmer still holds tightly to "evangelical," as do Campolo, Perkins, Wallis, and Sider. I believe if Skinner were still alive, he would too. And perhaps it's the fighter in me: I claim the name "evangelical." Then I explain: "You see, it was evangelicals who laid the foundation for women's suffrage. Oh, you didn't know that? Well, did you know they also galvanized labor unions and were largely responsible for the spread of the abolitionist movement? You'd never believe it today, but that's who we really are." That tells you a lot—how a movement is born. It all goes back to the movement's genesis. There you find its roots.

4

Broken Promises?

A Promise Keeper is committed to reaching beyond any racial and denominational barriers to demonstrate the power of biblical unity.
—Number Six of the Seven Promises of a Promise Keeper

What does PK think the role of women should be?

Promise Keepers believes that men and women are completely equal at the foot of the cross. Paul writes in Galatians 3:28, "There is neither Jew nor Greek, slave nor free, male nor female, for you are all one in Christ Jesus." As we continue to pursue reconciliation in the body of Christ, we believe unity in Christ transcends ethnic, social, and gender distinctions.
—Promise Keepers Web site

The year was 1997. Half a million men or more stood on the National Mall in Washington, DC. They sang, held hands, and listened to stories of struggle and triumph springing from the experiences of every major ethnic group in the United States. It was not Farrakhan's Million Man March. It was not a rally for gay pride. It was the Promise Keepers' Stand in the Gap Sacred Assembly, and the main issue of the day for this evangelical men's gathering was repentance for racism, abuse, and neglect.

It started with a conversation.

On March 20, 1990, Bill McCartney, award-winning football coach at the University of Colorado, sat at a Fellowship of Christian Athletes banquet with Dave Wardell. As the two men drove back to Denver together, McCartney turned to Wardell and asked, "What do you feel is the most important factor in changing a man spiritually, from immaturity to maturity?"[1]

"Discipleship," Wardell replied without missing a beat.

McCartney shared a vision with Wardell. What if fifty thousand men were to come together at the University of Colorado's Folsom Field to praise, worship, and receive teaching on what it takes to become mature followers of Jesus? The Promise Keepers' (PK) Web site explains that McCartney was imagining a revival among Christian men that would affect the health of families, their communities, and the marketplace. Revival-style events partnered with small-group discipleship structures became two hallmarks of the PK movement.

The model succeeded for a long time. From 1990 to 1995, PK event attendance increased each year. In 1995, PK reached 738,000 men at thirteen conferences in cities across the United States. Then, in 1996, PK decided racial reconciliation would become the ministry's primary focus for the year.

PROMISES OF RACIAL RECONCILIATION

McCartney's idea from the beginning was to call for racial reconciliation as a demonstration of the unity of the Christian community. In a 2007 interview, current PK president and CEO Tom Fortson, director of strategic alliances Gordon England, and national spokesman Steve Chavis discussed the group's history and mission.[2]

England recalled that during the last session of a long training day at PK's first big rally, Coach (as the leaders call McCartney) "felt the Lord confront him just before he went up to speak." Coach was a charismatic evangelical, which meant he experienced inspiration from the Holy Spirit, and he sometimes spoke out of his feeling of the Spirit's impromptu prompting. McCartney heard God ask, "What do you see?" He stood next to the stage looking at the group in the basketball arena and replied, "I see a bunch of Christian guys who are really excited about you!" God dug deeper; "What else do you see?" Coach replied, "They're mainly all white." With nearly thirty years of coaching behind him, McCartney was reared in the sports world—a world where diversity was the norm. The all-white crowd struck him as odd. Coach took the stage and explained the prompting he was feeling from God to the men, and he laid down the gauntlet:

> The Lord wants us to know that He is interested in men coming together in the name of his Son, but not just white men. He wants all men to come together, crossing boundaries. If we have this great idea to fill a stadium with mostly white men, we can all show up, but I do not believe He is going to pour out his spirit on us.[3]

Coach gave the men two charges that day: (1) invite twelve friends to next year's conference and (2) reach out and bring men of color with you next time.

Twenty-two thousand mostly white men convened at Folsom Field for the First National Men's Conference the following year. McCartney declared racial reconciliation a mandate of the movement, making it one of the seven promises of every Promise Keeper.

Promise Keepers developed eight Biblical Principles of Reconciliation to incorporate racial reconciliation into discipleship training. The organization constructed a division to focus exclusively on managing that value within the movement. Of these developments, Michael Emerson and Christian Smith wrote in *Divided by Faith*: "The Promise Keepers organization works hard to model racial reconciliation. Over thirty percent of its staff are persons of color, including people of all major racial groups."[4] The demographic makeup of PK's current board of directors demonstrates the organization's sustained commitment to this value: Three of five board members are men of color. Fortson is African American; Samuel Winder, chairman of the board, is a member of the Southern Ute tribe; and Dobie Weasel is a member of the Assiniboine, a Canadian First Nations tribe. In 1996, PK hired Raleigh Washington, co-author of *Breaking Down Walls: A Model for Reconciliation in an Age of Racial Strife* (1994), to lead the racial reconciliation division. Racial reconciliation was rolling to the forefront of the PK movement's agenda, becoming a major definer of what it means to be a follower of Christ.

In 1996, PK made racial reconciliation the theme of the year. They held twenty-two stadium conferences, and 1.1 million men nationwide were told racial reconciliation was a primary value of the gospel. This was the first time in evangelical history that a message of racial reconciliation was preached as a mandate of the gospel to such large audiences of pastors, organizational leaders, and ordinary Christian men.

This activity culminated on October 4, 1997, when PK hosted Stand in the Gap: A Sacred Assembly of Men on the National Mall in Washington, DC. On the heels of the African American Million Man March, PK convened an estimated five hundred thousand to one million men from across the United States, and racial reconciliation was a main topic of the day. C-SPAN carried the event live. My mother, an African American progressive, called me that day to ask if I was watching. She and my father sat riveted to their TV screen and listened to a Native American man preach from the podium on the National Mall about his faith in Jesus. It shocked and moved them.

That was the zenith of the PK movement. It was downhill from there.

The following year attendance at PK events dropped by more than 50 percent. McCartney reflected on the 1996 conferences in Emerson and Smith's *Divided by Faith*: "To this day, the racial message remains a highly charged element of Promise Keepers' ministry . . . of the 1996 conference participants who had a complaint, nearly 40 percent reacted negatively to the reconciliation theme. I personally believe it was a major factor in the significant falloff in PK's 1997 attendance—it is simply a hard teaching for many."[5]

What was so hard about this teaching? After all, PK's Eight Biblical Principles of Racial Reconciliation only covered the first of John Perkins's Three Rs. The principles advocated interpersonal reconciliation. Relocation and redistribution were never mentioned. Yet, even that bone caused white evangelical men to choke.

In his book *Sold Out*, McCartney tells the story of his

tours around the country to speak about racial reconciliation. During the tour McCartney lectured about his life as a coach and offered personal reflections on scripture to make the point that racial reconciliation was a necessity of the church, not an option. "But always," he writes, "when I finished there was no response—nothing. . . . In city after city, in church after church, it was the same story—wild enthusiasm while I was being introduced, followed by a morgue-like chill as I stepped away from the microphone."[6]

LIMITED PROMISES

That chill may have been trenchant resistance to change, or, more likely, it was an inability to grasp what McCartney was saying. People in groups can only take in as much as their worldview allows. Limited cultural tool kits prohibited Mc-Cartney's audience from comprehending the reality of systemic injustice. Accordingly, McCartney's audiences literally could not grasp imperatives two and three of the Three Rs.

When the last two of Perkins's Three Rs were not embraced as a goal within the Promise Keepers' curriculum on racial reconciliation, the movement forfeited the opportunity to speak prophetically and lay foundations for broadening the tool kits of white evangelical America. This failure raises the question of whether the absence of relocation and redistribution from the curriculum was PK's conscious choice or an oversight. In a recent interview, Emerson said he believed it was the result of the limited cultural tool kit of a white evangelical organization itself: "I would think they never even thought about it. Not that it's an oversight. Just that it doesn't seem important."[7]

When I asked PK's leaders why they chose not to communicate two of the Three Rs in their racial reconciliation message, the answer was simple: "We can't do it all."[8] England told the story of a meeting in 1992 between PK leaders and an ad hoc group of urban ministry practitioners. It occurred early in PK's development. At the meeting a member of John Perkins's Christian Community Development Association (CCDA) board spoke:

> His recommendation was that PK not seek to grow past the initial leadership rally, but rather seek to go deep. In other words, not seek to build an army, but build a Special Forces unit. There was some discussion about that. Some of the people responded by saying, "How this movement grows is really not about what we say about it, but about what God unfolds and where He brings it." [Others] responded saying, "There are groups for whom this is their single focus (i.e., John Perkins), and they unpack it and that's all they're working on. They're not working on marriage. They're not working on personal accountability of men. They're not doing evangelism. They're singularly focused on promise six and the other six promises are off the table." At that meeting, the [CCDA] fellow was lobbying for doing the thing that you're saying. But we should have done that only if we were just a reconciliation movement.[9]

A forced choice among strategies won the day in this discussion and is reflected in PK's final racial reconciliation strategy. Either PK would "do it all" in the Special Forces model or PK would focus where it could as it sought to build an army. To this day, that either/or thinking dominates the

PK leadership: "We can't do it all." "We're a men's movement, not only about reconciliation." "There are six other promises." There is a problem, though, with this line of reasoning. It is not reasonable. Emerson's critique and my question in the interview were not about what they *do*. It was about *the message*. It was about what they *say*. The problem was they didn't and they still don't *say* it all. If an *effective process* of racial reconciliation, even in its most simple form, requires three Rs—not one, not two, but three—then *the message* of racial reconciliation must also include three Rs. Nonetheless, Emerson speculates, PK seems unable to believe it is important for them to go deep in their teaching on the subject. Others can go deep. Depth of understanding and profound social change are not their calling. Instead of a Special Forces unit, they chose not just a wide army, as England put it, but an army ill-equipped to address the depth of reconciliation issues. The vast majority of the 3.5 million men who received PK's truncated teaching failed to attend John Perkins's CCDA conferences looking for more. The ill-equipped army quit before adequately achieving even the first R, even while they thought they had what they needed because the other two Rs were never even mentioned. They waged a campaign for interpersonal reconciliation, but failed to mount an adequate fight.

Perhaps the war paradigm itself was part of the problem. In war, leaders must resign themselves to casualties. The goal, therefore, becomes to increase the casualties on the side of the enemy while minimizing casualties of war on one's own side. If one runs with the war motif in the process of racial reconciliation, then casualties are acceptable. The generals must only decide how many casualties they can sustain within their own ranks and still win. The Christian Community Development Association representative may have seen the problem with the war motif in racial reconciliation. Discipleship is not primarily about warfare but about faithfulness to community and love for others. McCartney originally envisioned PK as a discipleship movement. Granted, in the evangelical worldview, very real spiritual warfare occurs along the discipleship journey. However, spiritual warfare is engaged for one ultimate purpose: to build up the body of Christ, the community of God. Thus discipleship is primarily about relationships and community development. Any casualties among the community of God ought to be utterly unacceptable, especially when it is clearly possible to avoid them. The ad hoc group that made an either/or choice transformed their session into a war-room debate, with generals discussing what casualties would be acceptable. In that meeting, two of the Three Rs became casualties of war, and with them died the hope of a true racial reconciliation movement springing from the Promise Keepers.

Promise Keepers rallies became cathartic events where white evangelicals pledged to take steps toward befriending men of color. This in itself was not bad or inappropriate—relational connection is a necessary first step forward for white evangelicals. PK had to start there, but they ended the message there. The lack of any further instruction on the requirements of racial reconciliation, including ending systemic and structural injustice, caused the racial reconciliation movement within PK to end unsuccessfully.

Emerson recounted the disillusionment of the post–PK racial reconciliation movement, on both sides. For the black men, who distrusted whites before the PK experience, the aftermath was worse. Emerson gave some examples: " 'Okay, they gave me a hug and told me they're sorry. Now they've disappeared.' Or 'Now I have twenty-eight white guys who want to be my buddy, but they don't want to know about what my people might be facing. They just want to go out to dinner.' Now there was distrust, exhaustion, and cynicism." "On the white side," Emerson continued, "I hear a lot of frustration like, 'I tried to reach out and I even thought we were connecting and becoming friends and then they stopped being interested'; or 'There was a disagreement and he didn't understand'; or 'It seems like I can't please him.' "[10]

Noel Castellanos, executive director of CCDA, spoke at PK rallies several times throughout the late 1990s. In our interview, Castellanos reminded me that Raleigh Washington, the leader of the Racial Reconciliation Division of Promise Keepers throughout the mid-1990s was a member of CCDA. Castellanos explained, "Washington clearly understood the Three Rs—a dynamic process that calls for interpersonal reconciliation, but also requires the actions of relocation and redistribution of resources." McCarthy's background, however, was in sports. While the sports world immersed him in multiethnic settings for thirty years of his life, his paradigm of racial reconciliation was formed more through the static lens of diversity. The 1992 conversation with the ad hoc urban ministry group sealed the strategic goal of PK. They were going to strive for "unity" in the church. In its simplest terms, this is evangelical-speak for "diversity"—the value of being together. This paradigm of unity does not take into account the process that unity requires.[11]

PRESSING FOR "PROCESS"

In my work as ethnic reconciliation specialist for InterVarsity Christian Fellowship–Southern California, I found that communities that conceived of ethnic reconciliation as a process involving personal sacrifice and suffering to achieve systemic change were far better prepared for the work ahead than those who conceived of ethnic reconciliation as diversity. Why? Diversity is about an end result. It is not about the difficult process that it takes to get there. True reconciliation is about a process that involves the whole person, all our relationships and all our interactions with the structures, systems, histories, and policies that govern our world. InterVarsity, like PK, is an evangelical organization that seeks to equip leaders to impact the church and the world. PK's focus is men. InterVarsity's focus is college students. Both conceive of themselves as movements. Yet unlike PK, there is no monolithic curriculum handed down from the top in InterVarsity structures. Instead, there are varieties of approaches within InterVarsity, even within a single region.

I served as director of ethnic reconciliation for InterVarsity–Greater Los Angeles for five years and then became a specialist who served all of Southern California in my last year with the organization. In that last year, I conducted a study of the state of ethnic reconciliation in all the InterVarsity chapters in Southern California. Chapters that conceived of reconciliation as a process prepared for that process with biblical foundations. Those foundations guided them through the process of relocating and redistributing resources and power within their structures. They also created structures and training to facilitate the process and equip its leaders. Those who conceived of reconciliation as diversity were unprepared for the suffering they experienced. They lacked biblical foundations to anchor them through the storms they encountered. They lacked structures to enable true social transformation rather than statistical or cosmetic changes. Generally speaking, they relied on one or two talks on the value of diversity per year and stopped there. Often, they justified this strategy with the mantra "We can't do it all."

Castellanos noted, "You could not be a part of PK from 1996 to 2000 and have conversations with Raleigh about the movement without talking about systemic justice, without talking about engaging, without talking about taking it further than having a black or white friend." Raleigh Washington was talking about a process that would take the value deeper throughout the PK movement, but his voice was destined to fall on unhearing ears. For he was pressing for the full "process," including systemic and structural reconciliation, within a white evangelical organization that conceived of reconciliation using its cultural tools: accountable freewill individualism, relationalism, and antistructuralism. They never engaged the full process and never thought it necessary.[12]

POLITICAL IMPLICATIONS OF FAILED PROMISES

The failure of PK's initiative on racial reconciliation affected the political allegiance of evangelicals. In the short run, the omission of systemic and structural change divided black and white evangelical America further. In the long run, though, it seems that the seeds of change planted in the mid-1990s may be sprouting in unexpected and surprising ways.

In the 2000 presidential election, only three years after the Stand in the Gap Sacred Assembly, black and white evangelicals split apart and voted overwhelmingly for opposing candidates. The Republican Party base, white evangelical men (many of whom attended PK events), cheered when their candidate was appointed to the Oval Office on the backs of hundreds of black citizens whose votes were never counted in Dade County, Florida. White evangelical men saw no connection between their relationship with the African American brother they hugged at a PK rally and the effect of their vote on the larger African American community. Few, if any, had relocated through the PK movement, and no one was challenged to redistribute resources at a personal or systemic level. Hence, when it came time to vote, the issue on white evangelicals' minds was singular, and it was not the call to end or curb or alleviate poverty or to love your ethnic neighbor as yourself in all spheres of life. These crucial issues had nothing to do with the white evangelical vote. The evangelical vote was about one thing—abortion.

George W. Bush was supported overwhelmingly by white evangelical voters because they knew that there would be multiple replacements needed for Supreme Court justices over the next eight years. They also knew that *Roe v. Wade* had no chance of being overturned if a Democrat won the presidency. White evangelicals cheered when Al Gore conceded the election. Black evangelicals mourned. They suffered a great loss. They endured a twenty-five-year setback with the effective nullification of the Voting Rights Act of 1964. They could see down the road and predict what was to come: a white evangelical president who did not know them and did not care that he did not know them. Worse, Bush would work against every major gain in the African American community of the past thirty years.

The predictions came true.

"*History* has prevented us from working together," Bush said in his thirty-three-minute speech to the NAACP in July

2006, his first address to the historic black organization. Yet, it was not just history. Bush made choices in the first years of his presidency that defined his relationship with the African American community. He crossed the boundaries between the executive and judicial powers to advocate for anti–affirmative action rulings in two Supreme Court cases. He pulled Colin Powell from the September 2001 United Nations conference against racism, in part to avoid discussions of reparations for slavery. He launched a war in Iraq that has created 33 percent of the nation's current debt. He authorized tax cuts for the nation's wealthiest citizens (increasing the debt by another 50 percent), then he advocated cuts to vital public services that make up only 1 percent of the debt.

The PK movement's reconciliation initiative had virtually no impact on white evangelical voting patterns in 2000 because it failed to broaden the white evangelical worldview. Its lack of focus on the Three Rs resulted in a different white evangelical vote from what might have been if they had broadened their message. Had they focused on all Three Rs, PK participants might have had more than one category on their minds when they entered the polling booth. A broader network with deeper ties within communities of color and historical and systemic analyses across racial lines might have broadened their worldview, enabling them to recognize the consequences of maintaining the status quo in the lives of their African American friends. They might have entered the voting booth with a different consciousness and awareness of racism.

According to Emerson and Smith's analysis, it would have taken short- or long-term relocation or immersion in networks of friends of color to alter the PK white evangelical worldview. PK focused on individual responses to racism through personal relationship alone. In predictable fashion, then, white evangelical men served as the voting base in 1994 that handed the House and Senate to the Republicans. White evangelical men also voted for George Bush overwhelmingly in 2000 and in 2004.

Emerson says it is reasonable, though, to suspect that the seeds of racial reconciliation that PK planted, as incomplete as they were, could be beginning to bear fruit more than ten years later.[13] For example, PK's board demonstrates a profound commitment to the value with three of five members being men of color. John Perkins credits the PK movement with opening the conversation for millions of evangelical Christian men who would not have heard the message otherwise.[14]

That PK raised the consciousness of white evangelical American men and said unequivocally "racial reconciliation is a mandate of the gospel" is significant in the scope of American history. While mainline churches, Catholics, and Jews launched multiple racial reconciliation initiatives in the civil rights era, evangelicals experienced no mass movement for racial reconciliation until the 1990s, and PK was the first evangelical group to bring the issue of racism into sharp focus on a massive scale. The movement exposed 3.5 million evangelical men to the most basic category of interpersonal reconciliation. It helped them identify their personal prejudice and offered these men, many of whom were or would become leaders in the church, the category of "repentance for the sin of personal prejudice." Through the PK movement, masses of white evangelical men were exposed for the first time to the concept that racism is not just a social problem. It is sin.

Emerson cautions, however, that a combination of factors was involved. PK's teaching deposited the category of interpersonal racial reconciliation into the general consciousness of evangelical America. However, at the time, white evangelical men still lacked networks of color that would challenge their worldview and deposit new tools into their cultural tool kit. Hence, their immediate attempts fell flat.

The overall browning of America, Emerson believes, has fostered the unintentional immersion of evangelical whites in networks of people of color, and this immersion may be having a similar affect as intentional immersion had in his 2000 study. He explains: "Since the immigration laws of the 1960s, we have more than tripled the minority percentage of the U.S. So, it's a whole different reality than it was in the 1960s, '70s and even '80s. . . . It then becomes something that you don't just read about. It's here. So, I need to understand what's going on and what it all means."[15] Many white evangelicals, particularly those living in urban centers, no longer have to uproot themselves to be immersed in networks of color. They find people and perspectives of color at work, in the marketplace, on television, and in church. According to Emerson, this input, along with current teaching from Sojourners, CCDA, InterVarsity's Urbana conferences, Rick Warren's calls to take justice seriously, the National Association of Evangelicals' stance in favor of environmental stewardship, and *Christianity Today*'s stand against torture, may be having synergistic impacts with PK's teaching.[16]

Brenda Salter McNeil, a racial reconciliation consultant based in Chicago, told the story of a man she encountered in the late 1990s at a reconciliation training session for a corporation in Colorado. The white middle-class man had just come from a Promise Keepers event. He had accepted Jesus as his personal Lord and Savior years before, but at the PK conference, he experienced a second conversion. Not long before that PK event, the man had entered a convenience store with his teenage son. The store owner seemed to be of Middle Eastern descent because of the way he was dressed. Brenda recounted the man's story: "To this day, he's not sure what possessed him, but he started singing a song that he made up. He sang it right in this Arab man's face. The man entitled the song 'Ahab to A-rab.' " This was in front of his son. At the end of the PK service, which the man attended with his son, the conveners gave an altar call. They invited all who needed to repent of their racism to come to the altar. "The man's son turned to him and didn't say anything other than this, 'You're gonna go down there, Dad, right?' And he knew right then and there what his son was talking about; he went down to the altar and he repented with tears streaming down his face."[17]

Second conversion experiences like this happened for millions of white evangelical men at PK racial reconciliation events. Men saw their own racist behaviors and confronted their personal feelings of racism. The problem, at the time, was the lack of a clear strategy for how these men would work out this new awareness in the course of their daily lives. There was no relocation. There was no redistribution. There were only attempts at friendships that fell flat. Perhaps, however, black and brown America arrived on the doorsteps of these white evangelical men in order to initiate immersion of white evangelicals in networks of color. Thus, perhaps when they see Barack Obama on Fox, CNN, or MSNBC and when they remember the devastation of Katrina, they are also remembering the teaching of men like Raleigh Washington,

John Perkins, Bill McCartney, Noel Castellanos, and Richard Twiss, the Rosebud Lakota leader of a North American Indigenous movement to embrace Jesus while maintaining a distinct cultural identity. Perhaps they are remembering their own tears. Just maybe they are equipped in this new era with at least one value they would not otherwise have had: "We must be racially reconciled."

NO PROMISES ABOUT GENDER

Promise Keepers is an evangelical men's movement, but the churches belong to women. David Murrow, author of *Why Men Hate Going to Church*, writes, "The pastorate is a men's club. But almost every other area of church life is dominated by women. . . . With the exception of men's events and pastoral conferences, can you think of any large gathering of Christians that attracts more men than women?" [18]

In the 1990s, evangelical America attempted to solve the riddle of the decline of male church attendance. John Eldridge attempted to solve the riddle with companion books, *Wild at Heart* and *Captivating*. These books called men and women to live in what he called their "complementarian" pre-Fall gender roles. [19] *Wild at Heart* claimed to uncover the soul of men: the male soul is dangerous. Every man desires to be a hero or a warrior. That is why men are turned off by the passivity of Christian piety. Eldridge and his wife Stasi explain in *Captivating* that women dream of being the beautiful princess swept into a great romantic adventure. Like Murrow and Eldridge, PK aimed to reignite the souls of men. Unlike the authors, PK launched more than a book. It ignited a movement. It was not the first evangelical men's movement.

Billy Sunday and the Men and Religion Forward Movement of 1911 and 1912 are among PK's forebears. Sunday, a professional baseball player turned evangelist, preached on the revivalist circuit at the turn of the twentieth century. In addition to preaching on the evils of intemperance, Sunday was the founder of "Muscular Christianity," a fundamentalist response to the women's suffrage movement of the late 1800s and early 1900s. Sunday demanded a remasculinization of the church and Christian iconography.[20] The Men and Religion Forward Movement also began in response to women's suffrage. This movement built on the teachings of Sunday and developed a male-only ministry model—by males for males. They declared, "Women have had charge of the Church work long enough."[21]

While calling for a remasculinization of the church and adopting a by-males-for-males structure, PK differed slightly from its predecessor movements. Rather than pressing for a completely masculine Christianity, they wanted to "have it both ways," according to sociologist Bryan W. Brickner. They called on men to "keep the emotive, traditionally feminine Jesus, and to reaffirm a masculine Jesus."

When I first logged on to the PK Web site, I wondered how they approached gender reconciliation and was struck by one thing. None of the seven promises address men's relationship to women. In the PK statement of faith, the sixth point reads: "All believers in the Lord Jesus Christ are members of His one international, multi-ethnic and transcultural body called the universal church. Its unity is displayed when we reach beyond racial and denominational lines to demonstrate the Gospel's reconciling power."[22] Gender reconciliation is not viewed as a way God displays his reconciling power, despite the reality that one of the first biblical relationships to shatter at the Fall in Genesis 3 was the relationship between men and women. Thus, if God was ever to display his full glory on earth, the broken relationship between men and women would have to be reconciled. Otherwise the reversal of the Fall would be incomplete.

As I examined the site, I sought evidence to indicate PK's focus on reconciliation was also translated into gender reconciliation, perhaps in the makeup of the board, perhaps in the statement of faith, perhaps in one of the seven promises. The value was not there. In my interview with Fortson, England, and Chavis, I asked why Promise Keepers lacks women in leadership. "Our focus is men," Fortson responded. But, he added, about 33 percent of PK volunteers and employees are women. "And our former chief financial officer was a woman."[23] Jackie Loh joined the PK executive team in 2005 and left in 2006. Ms. Loh declined a request for interview, stating, "I always abide by the biblical principle to forget what is behind and press on to the goal that is ahead (Phil. 3:13b)."[24]

When I asked the three leaders if there was a consistent practice of consulting women about the needs for growth in men, Fortson joked: "No question. I've been married for thirty-six years. I get a lot of counsel!" The men laughed. Fortson continued, "We get counsel and information from Women of Faith." Women of Faith is the largest conference for women in the United States, founded by Stephen Arterburn, an evangelical self-help guru, in 1996. It holds far less understanding of racial reconciliation than PK. Of nine conference speakers in 2007, only one was a woman of color, an African American. In addition, it is currently owned and operated by Thomas Nelson Publishers, home of John Eldridge's *Wild at Heart* book series, which, like PK, sought to address the problem of the dearth of men in the church. This set of enmeshed interests is a textbook formula for a nonchallenging consulting relationship on gender. It is a partnership to achieve shared goals, not a consulting relationship able to identify blind spots and strategies for growth in problems around gender.

In the face of this information, I asked, "It's clear that you do a lot to help men address relationships with their wives. There seems to be a lack of focus within the promises on men's relationships with women who are not their wives. I'm wondering if that's covered outside of the seven promises or if that might be a blind spot."

Fortson responded, "Are you talking about single men?"

"No, I'm talking about married men," I explained. "Really what I'm talking about is relationships with women with no connection to marriage. They may be in the workplace or the marketplace or just in everyday friendships between men and women."

The men were silent.

I explained further, "It seems that the goal of the organization when it comes to healing the relationship between men and women has been focused on healing the relationship between men and their wives."

Fortson broke in, "Yes, promise number four."

"Exactly," I affirmed. "But I'm wondering, what about the relationship between men and women who are not their wives? That gets into issues of gender and power and empowerment."

Fortson responded, "A large part of our audience is married men and men who have been remarried. We do address the issues of single men—the issue of purity. We deal with the issue of same-sex marriage. And respect for women is part of our teaching and part of a given theme for a given year. This issue of integrity rings out in all areas of a man's life and that includes the issue of high respect and regard for women."

I persisted and clarified my question by asking what led PK to focus on the marriage relationship, rather than on a more holistic attempt to heal relationships between men and women in a variety of relationships. For example, the Promise Keepers movement started in 1990, but in the 1970s a campaign was underway to pass the Equal Rights Amendment (ERA) to give equal rights to women and guarantee equal pay for equal work, and the women's movement was active throughout the 1980s.[25] "It seems to me," I noted, "that a movement dealing with the issue of men's integrity and healing in relationships between men and women would address the power dynamics between men and women in general, not just in the context of marriage. So, I'm wondering if that was ever addressed in general. And if not, then why?" England responded:

> Coming out of the women's movement, there was a lot of rhetoric and positions being espoused—scores of books. When we came into this, one of the strongest single verses that was used on the platform was Ephesians 5:21—the whole business of mutual submission. There's been a long, consistent line of teaching on "servant leadership" in terms of esteem and care for all women, not just the wife. So, in the teaching area there's been a lot of help in that area for men. I think one of our directives, coming out of the women's movement and the secular men's movement, was to help establish and build the man, in

terms of his leadership, first within his marriage. These other things are there. But they are not the front door to that discussion. It's not the primary point of contact, because a man's relationship to women in general will probably never be better than his relationship to his wife, his mother and his daughters.

The Promise Keepers' view of gender is grounded entirely in a post-Fall conception that focuses on the marriage relationship between husband and wife. It is not based on the Genesis 1:27–28 understanding that men and women were both made in God's image and both received the divine command to have dominion over the earth. The PK view of gender is also not based on the Genesis 2:18 understanding of proper power dynamics. When God said, "It is not good for man to be alone; I will make him a helper as his partner," the Hebrew word for "helper" (*e'zer*) is only used in two other contexts in scripture—both of them referring to a higher helper. *E'zer* is used to describe warriors who stand on the front lines of battle holding the shields that protect the regiment advancing behind. The Gospels use the same word in its Greek form (*boetheo*) to describe the help people receive from Jesus. Hence, if PK's conception of women was grounded in such passages, they would teach that God's original intent for women and men is to be mutual *protectors* of each other—and that's being generous. One could make a case, from the text itself, that women were created to protect men. Even that interpretation must be balanced by the Genesis 1 call for men and women to share equal dominion. Nowhere, pre-Fall, are women subordinated to men.

PK's post-Fall model for all proper gender dynamics reinforced the power dynamics of the consequences of the Fall in Genesis 3. That text describes the effect of the man's and woman's lack of trust in God. The effect is that the woman's husband "shall rule over" her. It is one thing to see this as a description. It is another thing entirely to see this as a prescription. If it were a prescription, it would be the way God *wants* gender relations to be—the way it *should* be. However, according to the text, it is neither a prescription nor a curse. Only the ground and the serpent are actually "cursed." The rest of the post-Fall world, with all its broken relationships, is God's description of the consequences of broken relationships with the creator of the world.

In the context of the New Testament's patriarchal culture, the Ephesians concept of "mutual submission" is a profound prescription. It deems women as more than property and worthy of being cared for and even submitted to. Within its historical context, this is revolutionary. In today's postsuffrage context, however, in which women are far from property, the paradigm does not hold the same prophetic weight as it may once have. In addition, the gender paradigm of mutual submission is problematic outside of the marriage relationship. The power dynamics do not translate. If one tries to take the post-Fall marriage relationship, where power dynamics are clearly stated in favor of the husband, who is "the head of the wife as Christ is the head of the church," and turn it into a general principle to follow in all relationships with women, then the logical outcome is the man becomes the "head" over all women—wife or not.

The traditional marriage relationship seems to be exactly what PK intends to promote in all relationships between women and men. England said, after all, a major focus of

PK's teaching has been *servant leadership*. He also said the movement aimed to establish men's leadership role *first* within marriage. Thus, PK is aiming to bring men back into their "proper" role as leaders of the household first and the world second.

As Brickner points out, "The Promise Keepers have a dilemma. Women are not only the wives of pastors, but in contemporary Christian culture, they are also pastors. Women have their own congregations. They are ordained ministers. They are church leaders." I add they are CEOs and presidents and executive directors. How should a Promise Keeper interact with his woman pastor or his woman president? Should he offer her esteem and care? Some female executives might appreciate that, if the Promise Keeper offered the same to a male CEO. Somehow, though, I doubt that esteem and care is as satisfying or as reconciling in the boardroom as the offering of respect. Ephesians 5:21 tells men to esteem and care for their wives. Genesis 1 and 2 suggest men should respect women as equals in general, making it clear they were created for co-dominion with men on earth. Galatians 3:28 asserts the same equality for Christian communities.

Emerson explains that the problem with PK's work on gender is the limitation of using a singular relationship to determine all relationships to women as a universal prescription for an entire group of human beings. For conservative Christians who use marriage to define all male and female relationships, it is impossible to conceive of women as the boss, the president, the one in charge who should be obeyed, or half the workforce. Conservatives cannot see women as a general category.[26] As a result, PK sees gender dynamics through the framework of individuals and particular relationships. As a predominantly white evangelical organization, its cultural tool of relationalism orients it to husband-wife and family relationships. The PK kit lacks the tool to conceive of the issue in terms of general gender constructions and categories. As Emerson notes, "This makes sense if we use the tool kit metaphor. As carpenters are limited to building with the tools in their kits (hammers encourage the use of nails, drills encourage the use of screws), so white evangelicals are severely constrained by their religio-cultural tools."[27]

If PK's primary mission is the health of the whole community of God, it must address the weaknesses of men within that community. Because PK's primary constituency is white evangelical men and white males are the dominant group in the United States, the call to gender impartiality (Galatians 3:28) should be a major factor in achieving that mission. However, the white evangelical cultural tool kit limits PK's ability to remedy problems of gender in community. Promise Keepers will need the partnership of organizations and mentors with the cultural tools to understand and address gender discrimination within the church.

CONCLUSION

In both the cases of race and gender, the Promise Keepers approached the problems of men using the only cultural tools they had: individualism, relationalism, and antistructuralism. The results were a truncated and ineffective response to racism and no engagement with issues of gender within evangelical America. The seeds of racial reconciliation were planted in the mid-1990s, and it may be that they are beginning to bear fruit ten years later, but the question still remains: what kind of fruit will these seeds bear? While it is true that PK's board demonstrates a profound commitment to diversity and promise six still affirms the need for interpersonal racial reconciliation, would PK followers advocate systemic changes necessary to bring about the redistribution of power and resources in society? Would these evangelicals support what John Perkins calls a biblical mandate for creative and effective reparations for African enslavement on U.S. soil? Seeds can only produce fruit from their kind. The seeds planted by the PK movement in the 1990s could not bear such fruit.

In the gender arena, PK focused on the relationships of men with the women in their families, especially husbands with wives. PK was unable to comprehend women in roles and relationships with men beyond this limited sense. This limitation, in turn, focused on men's relationship to their wives as leaders. This is not gender reconciliation, which would directly address power dynamics from a biblical perspective between men and women beyond the family and in the larger society.

Again, the seeds planted will determine the fruit borne. Thus, the question persists: what fruit of gender reconciliation will PK's seeds bear in the arena of politics and public policy? Their post-Fall understanding of power dynamics in gender relationships foreshadows failure in gender reconciliation. PK recruited three and a half million men into a gender paradigm that demotes women to followers in all male/female relationships. This approach to gender translates into inaction or opposition toward policies that focus on the empowerment of women. In 1984, the National Association of Evangelicals (NAE) released a statement opposing the Equal Rights Amendment (ERA). The NAE feared the legislation's larger implications on abortion, women in military combat, and the denial of tax-exempt status "to any school, seminary, or church which believes that God has ordained different roles for men and women."[28] The seeds planted by the PK movement only reinforce this political position on women's roles in society and in the church. Thus, the status quo among Promise Keeping white evangelical men will remain, and fruit borne in gender reconciliation will originate from another source, not PK.

What, then, is needed for PK and evangelical organizations like it to grow in the areas of race and gender reconciliation? First, and most important, there must be desire for growth and change. I sensed that desire in the hearts of the PK men. At one point, Gordon England confessed, "You have to remember, we were drinking from a fire hose." England acknowledged they didn't get everything right. Fortson, the Promise Keepers president, thanked me in the end, saying, "Those are good questions you asked. It helped us to take a second look at our effectiveness and what we teach. So, this has been very helpful to us."[29]

After desire, a posture of humility is necessary. Evangelicals ground their understanding of humility in the example of Jesus in Philippians 2:5–8. In that passage, Jesus demonstrates humility in that, while he was God, he did not grasp at power; rather, he humbled himself and became obedient— even to death on a cross. In other words, humility leads those with power to let it go for the sake of the other. Humility helps powerful people face their blind spots, admitting that they have them and that they are a problem.

After desire and humility, displacement is the next step.

In both arenas, race and gender, it will be necessary for the PK leaders and other movements who identify with their plight to immerse themselves in communities or networks with the cultural tools they lack. This is the most important path white evangelicals and historically white evangelical organizations must take on the path to expanded cultural tool kits and an expanded worldview. For PK, it might mean approaching CCDA again and asking forgiveness for the way its representative's comments were disregarded back in the early 1990s. It might also mean requesting mentoring relationships with CCDA board members and affiliates. In the area of gender, it might mean seeking to expand its worldview by engaging in a process of listening to the thoughts and theologies of women leaders outside of the proscribed PK network. Fortson might call on Mimi Haddad, the evangelical executive director of Christians for Biblical Equality and request a mentoring relationship in this area.

Finally, the temptation of those with power entering the world of the other will be to reclaim power through teaching, helping, or fighting a worldview shift. The most important action necessary at this stage is the act of listening. Hearing the stories of the other, listening to their views of Jesus, listening to the scriptures that have brought healing and renewal of faith in their lives, and listening to one's own heart as it faces its own culpability—these are potent acts. They are reconciling acts. But the journey does not end here.

Once worldview shifts, those with power must make a decision. The next phase is the most difficult and most costly: redistribution of power and resources. This is what was lacking in the 1990s and it is still lacking. To turn a corner, this must be addressed in both arenas, race and gender.

If Promise Keepers wants to strengthen the church

through men's discipleship, then there is no greater scripture it can model and teach than "God has told you, O mortal, what is good; and what does the Lord require of you, but to do justice and to love mercy and to walk humbly with your God?" (Micah 6:8).

5

Apologies and Power Politics

When you are offering your gift at the altar, if you remember that your brother or sister has something against you, leave your gift there before the altar and go; first be reconciled to your brother and sister, and then come and offer your gift.

—Jesus, Matthew 5:23–24

On June 20, 1995, the largest Protestant denomination in the United States did something the nation has yet to do. The Southern Baptist Convention issued a formal apology for its role in upholding and benefiting from the evils of slavery and racism in the United States. The apology acknowledged the denomination's role in participating in, supporting, and acquiescing to the "particularly inhumane nature of American slavery."[1]

The Southern Baptist Convention was born in 1845. As evangelical abolitionists gained traction, slavery divided the church as much as it divided the nation. Large denominations, such as the Methodists, Presbyterians, Episcopalians, and American Baptists, split into Northern and Southern parts. The Southern contingent of the American Baptists wanted to retain the right to send slave-owning missionaries to Native Americans. The Northern Baptists would not allow it, so the Southerners formed their own denomination. The two groups became the Northern and Southern Baptist Conventions. Within ten years, the Southern Baptists outnumbered the Northern denomination.

The 1995 resolution admitted that Southern Baptists failed, in many cases, "to support, and in some cases opposed, legitimate initiatives to secure the civil rights of African Americans." It acknowledged that racism had divided the Southern Baptists, separated them from African Americans, and distorted Christian morality, "leading some Southern Baptists to believe that racial prejudice and discrimination are compatible with the Gospel."[2]

The Southern Baptist Convention has a mixed history. Since the turn of the twentieth century, the convention has issued periodic calls for Southern Baptists to refrain from racist acts such as lynching and mob violence. However, in many cases, Southern Baptists upheld racist institutions and defended racist practices. One stark example comes from the Southern Baptist Declaration of 1954 and the subsequent response of the Mississippi Southern Baptists.

Since the 1940s, when J.B. Weatherspoon, professor of ethics at Southern Baptist Theological Seminary, became the board chair of the Southern Baptist Christian Life Commission, the commission has pursued an agenda marked by concern for social issues, including racism.[3] In response to the Supreme Court ruling in the case of *Brown v. Board of Education of Topeka*, the progressive Christian Life Commission issued a report in support of the decision. The commission said it was "in line with the constitutional guarantee of equal freedom to all citizens, and with the Christian principles of equal justice and love of all men."[4] The commission's report had three dissenting views: W.M. Nevins, a pastor from Kentucky, who raised the specter of mixed blood descendents; Arthur Hay, a dentist from Albuquerque, who insisted that white blood must be kept pure; and William Douglas Hudgins, pastor of First Baptist Church of Mississippi and a rising star within the convention, who simply cast his vote in opposition—without comment.

The next day Hudgins preached that the church had no business engaging in affairs of the state, indicating he took a neutral stance on the issue of race. Nine years later, though, during the Summer Project of 1964, Hudgins's congregation voted to "confine its assemblies and fellowships to those other than the Negro race, until such a time as cordial relationships could be *reestablished*" (emphasis added). This wording was deceptive. The last time the congregation had any *established* fellowship with an African American was when they removed the last one from the church in 1868 to allay fears of Reconstruction.[5]

In spite of the declaration, segregation was still accepted as a divinely ordained norm by a large contingent of Southern Baptist churches. In fact, Jerry Falwell's church, Thomas Road Baptist Church, "adhered to strict closed-door policies," according to historian Charles Marsh. Marsh dedicates a full chapter in *God's Long Summer* to the impact of Hudgins's theology on the segregationist movement:

> It is no exaggeration to say that one can simply not understand white indifference to black suffering and liberation during the civil rights movement without understanding the religion of William Douglas Hudgins. There are meaningful differences between the revered and genteel minister to Jackson's political

and social elites and the seething Imperial Wizard of the White Knights of the Ku Klux Klan. Nonetheless, the success of [their] violent mission depended largely on the kind of Gospel Hudgins eloquently preached to white Christians in the spacious sanctuary of the First Baptist Church and over the airwaves of the state and throughout the South.[6]

While the Christian Life Commission (CLC) was progressive in its views, its structures generally were not. Then, in 1973, the CLC announced a resolution that galvanized the ire of conservatives already irate about its stances on race. The commission issued a statement in favor of the *Roe v. Wade* Supreme Court decision. While the Religious Right in general did not pick up *Roe v. Wade* until the 1980s as its lightning-rod issue, the Southern Baptist Convention was torn apart by the pro-choice resolution. Cultural conservatives already ignited by the race issue were utterly galvanized by *Roe v. Wade.* As the Right rose to power throughout the 1980s, so too did the conservative bloc within the Southern Baptist Convention, until, finally, they won power.

Richard Land's voice boomed through the receiver of my cell phone. He described, with a Texas drawl, the situation when he took over leadership of the CLC—now renamed the Ethics and Religious Liberty Commission: "When I was elected as head of this commission in 1988, I was the first clear, open, undeniably conservative agency head. I was at ground zero of the conservative resurgence within the Southern Baptist Convention."[7] At forty-one, Land was the youngest of the conservative players brought to power. He replaced Foy Valentine, whose "liberal" affiliations with the Religious Coalition for Abortion Rights (RCAR) and the American Civil Liberties Union (ACLU) resulted in his ouster. The one thing Land and Valentine could agree on, however, was the race issue.[8]

In seminary, Land explains, "I was considered a 'rank liberal' on the race issue and was very difficult to categorize for some of my friends because I was a theological conservative and was very 'liberal' on the race issue."[9] Land grew up in segregated Houston at the height of the civil rights movement. He considered Dr. King a personal hero and a model of Christian activism. "I was always raised to believe," Land explains, "that racism was not only wrong, it was sin. That part of our society was simply sinful and wrong, and that under no circumstances as a Christian was I to treat anyone any differently because of the color of their skin."[10] Land feels a personal connection to King:

> You know, we all have pet peeves; we all have certain things that get under our skin. Well, one of my pet peeves has been and is bigots. I just find it hard to love bigots. I know God loves them, but it's hard for me to. Dr. King helped me with that. I remember him saying, "Those that you would change you must first love." And I thought, you know, if Dr. King can love Bull Conner, I can love Bull Conner. If Dr. King can love Sheriff Jim Clark, I can love Sheriff Jim Clark.[11]

Land was a strong supporter of the Voting Rights Act of 1964 and the Civil Rights Act of 1965. When he entered the presidency of the transitioning Ethics and Religious Liberty Commission, one of the first things he did was to hold a conference on racial reconciliation. He wanted "to make it clear that going from a liberal to a conservative did not mean *any* difference on that issue—that this was not an issue of Right or Left; it was an issue of right or wrong."[12] Land called Valentine and asked him to be a speaker at the conference: "I said, 'Now, my friends are going to be mad at me for inviting you, and your friends are going to be mad at you if you accept. But this issue is bigger than our friends.' And he said, 'I agree, Richard, and I'll do it.' " Land was right: "[Valentine] had friends writing him letters and yelling at him on the phone, and I had my friends—I mean, I'm holding the phone away from my ear because people are yelling at me over the phone."[13]

Land followed up the conference with a private, off-the-record "consultation"—a common way for Southern Baptists to work through complex issues. This one was on racial reconciliation. Land invited fifteen African American Southern Baptist pastors and fifteen white Southern Baptist pastors for this off-the-record discussion. He described the meeting to me:

> We met that night, and the next morning we got together and the person who had been elected as the spokesperson for the African American group said, "Dr. Land, I hope you understand that you white folks are very complicated people. You don't always mean what you say, and you don't always say what you mean. So we caucused last night, and we came to the conclusion that you really mean what you say, so we're going to tell you the truth." So they did.
>
> Part of what they said to us was, "You don't understand how badly you have hurt us. We don't mean you, personally. We mean white Christians. It's

one thing to be discriminated against and to be treated badly by whites; it's another thing to be discriminated against and treated badly by Christian brothers."[14]

Land's tinny drawl focused down to laser-point precision through the receiver:

> You know, that statement sort of rummaged around inside my heart and my brain for a while, and I realized that we had passed numerous resolutions condemning racism—in fact, the convention's record on this is not that bad.
>
> In 1946 we passed our first resolution condemning unfair treatment of "colored people" and called for them to be treated fairly and justly. We had passed resolutions—on average, two or three a decade—condemning racism and condemning racist activities. But what we had never done was to accept personal responsibility as a convention for having supported slavery, for having supported Jim Crow and segregation, and empowering those who had been victimized by apologizing and asking for forgiveness.[15]

The 1995 resolution was a new moment in racial reconciliation for the Southern Baptists. It lamented and repudiated "historic acts of evil such as slavery from which we continue to reap a bitter harvest." The denomination recognized that racism today was inextricably tied to the past. And, the Southern Baptists apologized to all African Americans for "condoning and/or perpetuating individual and systemic racism in our lifetime." They repented "of racism of which we have been guilty, whether consciously (Psalm 19:13) or unconsciously (Leviticus 4:27)."[16] In early 1989 Land began to seek a venue for the first steps toward reconciliation:

> We had a problem we had to deal with, which was that the liberals in our convention and the moderates in our convention were trying to get a resolution passed in which we "repented" of slavery and racism. Well, there's a theological problem for Southern Baptists with that, because we don't believe that we can repent for our ancestors. We can't. We can express regret and apologize, but repentance for Southern Baptists concerns spiritual issues and concerns personal relationship with God. For example, I have a great-great-grandfather who was a slaveholder. Well, I'm sorry for that, and I grieve over the fact that he was so blind on this issue, but I can't repent for him. He has to deal with God, had to deal with God, on his own. I mean, we're not Mormon; I can't repent for dead ancestors.[17]

The resolution further resolved that Southern Baptists asked their African American brothers and sisters to forgive them. They committed themselves "to eradicate racism in all its forms from Southern Baptist life and ministry."[18]

Land, energized, words at a clip, continued to explain events that led to this historic resolution. He said that he noticed that the Southern Baptists were meeting in Atlanta in 1995 to celebrate the sesquicentennial of their founding. He went to Jim Henry, president of the convention, and said:

Mr. President, we have a great heritage, and we certainly have the right to celebrate it. But we've also got some real ugly laundry in the closet, and we have to deal with the family laundry in the closet, otherwise it's just unseemly. And so I'm going to ask you to suspend the rules [that prohibited consideration of a resolution until the second day of the convention] by presidential edict, and that you allow us to print and to consider a resolution before we have our celebration.

Henry agreed.[19]

They dealt with the resolution the afternoon before their sesquicentennial celebration. The vote was 98 percent in favor. Land noted that perhaps one and a half to two percent felt that they were casting aspersions upon their ancestors, whom they regarded as godly people. Land replied to them, "Well, many of them *were* godly people, but this was sin, and they had a blind spot, and their blind spot was race. And we have to acknowledge that. And we have to acknowledge the hurt and the damage that it caused."[20]

The resolution committed Southern Baptists to pursuing racial reconciliation in all their relationships.[21] Its final paragraph declared:

Be it finally RESOLVED, That we pledge our commitment to the Great Commission task of making disciples of all people (Matthew 28:19), confessing that in the church God is calling together one people from every tribe and nation (Revelation 5:9), and proclaiming that the Gospel of our Lord Jesus Christ is the only certain and sufficient ground upon which redeemed persons will stand together in restored family union as joint-heirs with Christ (Romans 8:17).[22]

Land was on the platform throughout the debate, and as he looked out over the nearly twenty thousand mostly white delegates, another thing became clear. The racial socioeconomic structure of Atlanta at the time was observable in the hotel's staff. Almost everyone in a service position was African American. And throughout the convention, the hotel service staff gave no indication they were the least bit interested in its business, except during the debate on the resolution. "During that debate," Land explains, "no refreshments were being served, no halls were being swept, no chairs were being moved. The people that were there, watching, who were African American, were watching us and were listening intently to our debate."[23]

The *New York Times* reported the next day, "During the brief discussion that preceded the vote, Gary Frost, a black pastor from Ohio who was elected last year as the denomination's first vice president, appealed to the crowd: 'I believe it is up to the body of Christ, the church of Jesus Christ, to begin true reconciliation. I pray that you accept this resolution.'"[24]

OFFERING HOPE

According to Land, the resolution "did lance the boil. . . . It's one of the reasons we now have about 750,000 African American Southern Baptists."[25] The resolution lanced the boil because it offered hope. The *New York Times* reported in the same article that Calvin O. Butts III, pastor of the 4,500-

member Abyssinian Baptist Church in Harlem called it "a marvelous statement."[26] Butts said, "If there's a fitting response to the 'Letter from Birmingham Jail,' this is it," referring to King's famous 1963 appeal to white southern clergy to support the civil rights movement.[27]

Others, however, were skeptical. Arlee Griffin Jr., pastor of 4,000-member Berean Missionary Baptist Church in Brooklyn, took a doubtful view, calling the resolution only a first step, and saying that in racial matters, Southern Baptists have "a long history and legacy to overcome." Griffin, who served as historian for the Progressive National Baptist Convention, a separate denomination, went on, "It is only when one's request for forgiveness is reflected in a change of attitude and actions that the victim can then believe that the request for forgiveness is authentic." He said he wanted to see the denomination integrate substantially its leadership, agency staffs, and seminary faculties.[28]

I was in accord with Rev. Butts at the time of the resolution. I was hopeful because I saw the shift happening throughout evangelical America. Evangelicals were beginning to deal with racism. That hope rose again as I conducted my interview with Land. The wording of that resolution is not like the message of the Promise Keepers. It includes admission of the culpability of Southern Baptists in the systemic evils of slavery and racism in the United States. It promised "commitment to eradicate racism in all its forms from Southern Baptist life and ministry."[29] All its forms include the culture and mission of the convention; its rules and structures; and its political life and ministry. It also includes interpersonal forms of racism, such as racially separate congregations and unequal resources distributed to churches. I was also hopeful because the man who wrote the resolution, who was so excited that it passed, also held a position with the power to make real changes in the convention.

When I asked my next question of Land, I was still hopeful:

> HARPER: What work has the convention done since then, in the area of race and social justice?
>
> LAND: We quit focusing on the "white donuts" around our major urban areas, and started focusing on the urban areas. And we have, on average, founded a predominantly African American Southern Baptist Church, in a predominantly African American part of our major cities, at the rate of one a month since 1995. We have been founding churches, committing resources to founding churches, committing resources for scholarships among African American students for scholarships to our seminaries, etc.
>
> HARPER: Interesting. In your area—in particular, in policy—are there ways that you are able to enact or to move racial reconciliation forward into practice by fighting for policies that matter to the black community?
>
> LAND: Well, we focus more on racial reconciliation on the local level. We have a lot of state conventions that do joint mission projects, for instance, that go and work together with blacks to build black churches or to build churches together or do mission projects together. We have been focusing on building relationships with and among the African American and the Anglo communities.[30]

As often happens with well-intentioned practices, what Land described has had unintended consequences. One person, whom I will call "Jack," told me about his black Southern Baptist Church and its experience of life and ministry within the convention. Jack's church is three years old. He is white and his pastor is African American. The pastor founded the church intending it to be multiracial. The church is about 50 percent African American, 25 percent Hispanic and 25 percent white. Jack is the only deacon at his church, so he and his pastor are very close:

> If you talk to my pastor, the frustration grows and grows and grows and grows in him and in me. And that frustration is: one, we were told where we had to put the church. It had to be in an area that was dying, because that's considered the inner city and that's what a black pastor does. So we're put into this poor area. Two, we talked to many other Southern Baptist pastors who started churches at the same time— white pastors. Our pastor and our church [are] getting not even half of what these other churches are getting. . . . Our membership is young folks who are the working poor, so of course our offerings are not very much. Our offerings are small, but the needs are great. We're still stuck in a storefront—three years later. We don't have enough space.

With exasperation, Jack continues, "It's just like they set you up to fail! And then, three, we watch when they start a white congregation. They send them to the suburbs with two hundred people from the church it's coming out of. And they're getting lots of resources. And before you know it, they've got a building up."[31] A thick cloud of despair settled over our interview and with it came a moment of silence.

I thought back to my interview with Land, who explained that his office supported the reauthorization of the Voting Rights Act of 1965, which provides protection of minorities' right to vote. The convention also issued strong support in favor of welfare reform, according to Land:

> I think most fair-minded people would argue that welfare reform has been at least a mitigated success and certainly has been far preferable to what preceded it, which was a welfare system that was destructive to the people it was trying to help in terms of dependency and having people into the third generation on welfare.[32]

The Urban Institute, a DC-based public policy think tank, held the Welfare Reform Roundtable: Reviewing a Decade, Previewing the Future, in July 2006, marking the tenyear anniversary of the passing of the legislation. Participants included a long list of writers and critics who generally hailed the legislation as a necessary bipartisan step forward from the previous system. Consensus held that the old system trapped families in a cycle of generational impoverishment, while the new system helped cut the number of families on welfare virtually in half and helped those families make the transition from generational impoverishment to hope. On the other hand, the consensus was also strong that there were large numbers of families for whom the system did not work. Rather than helping them, the system left these families with children in poverty.[33]

Land was able to point to two pieces of legislation his office campaigned for over the past eleven years that directly addressed African Americans issues—just two. Close inspection of the Ethics and Religious Liberty Commission's 2007 legislative agenda illuminates the disparity between the radical antiracist stance the convention promised in its resolution and the soporific state on the ground. The focus of the SBC's legislative agenda is almost exclusively on issues that affect the individual's personal well-being and morality: sanctity of human life, homosexuality, health, judges, and immigration. With respect to personal morality, white and African American Baptists are not far apart in their values. The National Baptist Convention, USA, is a historically black denomination; in a January 2007 survey of 885 members, 55 percent of respondents took a culturally conservative view on issues of personal morality. The majority of respondents said they did not believe one could be a Christian and support a woman's right to choose, approve of same-sex marriage, or believe in both creationism and evolution.[34] These personal moral issues, however, do not define the political platforms that shape this historically black denomination.[35] The president of the National Baptist Convention, USA, and pastor of the White Rock Baptist Church in Philadelphia, William J. Shaw, wrote a position paper leading up to the 2004 presidential election that outlined the issues important to the denomination: a moratorium on the death penalty, reexamination of the Three Strikes and You're Out bill with preference for intervention/prevention strategies over incarceration, advocacy for a No Dollars Left Behind policy to match President Bush's No Child Left Behind policy, and steps to ensure fair and accurate voter registration practices.[36] In a recent interview, Shaw added health care to the list of prime issues facing African Americans.[37]

What is the SBC Ethics and Religious Liberty Commission doing to address the legislative priorities of its large African American constituency? When asked that question, Land repeated: the convention is building more black churches.

Michael Emerson shared his thoughts on the matter:

> There is this sense that "We welcome nonwhite folk into our fold and we're very proud when they do come, but we know best. We know what our faith is. So, you may bring up other issues, but we have to discount those." Certainly the black churches they're bringing in are concerned with abortion and gay rights, but I'm sure they're concerned with a whole lot more too. So, why don't they go *there*? *There* is who they're becoming.[38]

I suspect the reason the SBC does not go *there* is because they do not think they have to. The Southern Baptist Convention took its prophetic stance on principle, as a result of Richard Land's measured immersion into a network of black pastors (the off-the-record consultation). It did not come from deep understanding of the issues as the result of long-term immersion in networks of color. Rather, the SBC has been overwhelmingly white since its inception. So, its white evangelical worldview has been reinforced again and again for a century and a half.[39] This worldview, as we saw in chapter 4, has three major cultural tools: accountable freewill individualism, relationalism, and antistructuralism. Hence, they gravitate toward political issues that focus on individual morality.

The Southern Baptist Convention pursued racial reconciliation through a *transactional* approach like the understanding of salvation Dallas Willard called "bar-code faith," explained in chapter 1. Once a sinner repents of his sins and accepts Jesus as his Lord and Savior, the deal is done. Jesus pays the legal penalty for the sinner's sin through his death on the cross and the sinner's soul is saved. From that point on, nothing can threaten the believer's salvation.

The Southern Baptist Convention approached racial reconciliation with the same "bar-code" paradigm with which it viewed salvation. Once the convention apologized for its culpability in slavery and racism, the transaction was complete. The slate was wiped clean and the convention was, in a spiritual sense, saved. From that point on, any white evangelical actions to move forward were simply a sign of their benevolent largess toward African Americans, proof they were "good Christians," no matter how small or inconsequential the actions. For "bar-code faith," actions have nothing to do with salvation. The declaration of faith alone saves.

Racial reconciliation does not work this way. Perkins's Three Rs require not only interpersonal reconciliation, but also economic, systemic, and political redistribution of resources, as well as relocation into the world and experiences of those who experience racism. The transactional paradigm led the Southern Baptist Convention to fall short on each of these points. First, its strategy of focusing on building black churches in black areas perpetuates the cycle of separate and unequal churches and hinders the ability of Southern Baptist parishioners to build networks of relationships across color lines. To build cross-racial networks, they must first dismantle a church-growth strategy that has maintained their former thick de facto color lines. Second, while the convention might point to the focus on building black churches as a clear redistribution of resources, this is not an *equitable* redistribution of resources. Their policy mandates that new black churches be planted in blighted urban areas without the necessary funding to build those churches beyond bare survival, which institutionalizes inequitable distribution of resources and widens the gap between black and white churches. What's more, the denomination has failed to address the needs and issues of the churches of color within the convention. Finally, the denomination may perceive itself as "relocating" because of its commitment to plant black churches. In reality, however, black pastors who build black churches in black ghettos are the ones "relocating." The SBC has no measure in place to press for nonblack laity and pastors to relocate to urban centers or for black pastors and laity to reach out beyond the ghetto.

A relational, rather than transactional, theology of salvation would be more helpful to the Southern Baptist pursuit of reconciliation. Relationship is about love, not about a one-time legal transaction. Love requires focused attention to the desires, needs, and concerns of the other. It goes out of its way to understand and serve the other and expects any relationship to change both parties and the way they do life together. In addition, trust can be broken in a relationship, thus risking the integrity of the relationship. Racial reconciliation must be approached as requiring interpersonal, personal, political, and systemic changes on behalf of the other as part of the process of sustaining relationships. In short, Christians should expect to be utterly changed in our pursuit of racial reconciliation. "Bar-code" theology holds no such expectation.

William J. Shaw noted in our interview that members of the Southern Convention, like those in other predominately white bodies, may have some genuine regret for the social stances that they took, but the test of their resolve to achieve racial reconciliation is whether or not they will work to reverse the inequities that developed out of those stances. Shaw observed, "That's a painful thing for those who helped to establish the inequities. They benefited from the inequity. To lose those benefits is a painful thing." He concluded that the test of their resolve is therefore whether or not Christians are willing to have their pain increased to eliminate the sources of pain that have caused so much suffering to so many people.

The Southern Baptist Convention's lack of attention to policies and political issues of concern to its African American parishioners is both a symptom of their transactional paradigm of racial reconciliation and the outcome of more than 150 years of racial homogeneity. Their long-standing white networks reinforce a worldview that causes the SBC to favor legislation focused on individual personal health and morality, not on the well-being of an entire group of people different from themselves, whom their tradition has oppressed.

POWER POLITICS

The equality that the Southern Baptist Convention tried to deliver to blacks was taken away from women. On the heels of its 1995 apology, the Southern Baptist Convention enacted, by democratic vote, a new statement of faith called the Baptist Faith and Message (BFM) that set the stage for the subjugation of women within the convention. In 1998, the denomination's delegates voted to change the BFM to include a call for women to submit to their husbands in the home. Then in 2000, the delegates voted to amend the BFM again. This time they included the stipulation that "the office of pastor is reserved for men."[40] At the time only thirty-one of forty-one thousand senior convention pastors were women. There was no threat to the status quo of male rule. From 1845 to 1998, the denomination had only made two revisions in BFM. Then in two years, it made two revisions, both focused on the role of women, an issue which the denomination had never addressed before.[41]

We saw a similar pattern in the tactics of the Promise Keepers. Both PK and the Southern Baptist Convention took limited and inadequate steps toward racial reconciliation, and in both cases, PK and the SBC took no action toward gender reconciliation. Instead, they defined women in terms of marriage and subordinated them. Yet the Southern Baptist Convention went further; they actively limited the influence and leadership capacity of women within their denomination by excluding women from ordination as pastors.

In an article for *Christian Ethics Today*, William E. Hull, pastor of Mountain Brooke Baptist Church and research professor at Samford University, said: "These novel amendments so recently enacted have long been controversial and even divisive within our Baptist fellowship."[42] He points out that multiple groups within the convention have had long histories of emphasis on the complete equality of women within the church. In fact, the standard practice of the convention had been to exclude divisive points from the BFM because it was intended to be a consensus-building document. This time, though, Hull explains:

> The architects of BFM 2000 made its adoption an exercise in the politics of exclusion. Rather than both sides studying the issue together and seeking to resolve our differences by patient investigation and friendly dialogue, a decision was made to cut off discussion and settle the matter decisively, not by

deeper study of the Biblical evidence or by weighing the merits of divergent viewpoints, but by majority vote of assembled messengers [delegates].[43]

The Southern Baptist Convention Web site states that it made the changes to the BFM "to address the 'certain needs' of our own generation. In an age increasingly hostile to Christian truth, our challenge is to express the truth as revealed in Scripture, and to bear witness to Jesus Christ, who is 'the Way, the Truth, and the Life.' "[44] Thus, they frame the measure as a defense of the truth against a hostile world. This posture is typical of fundamentalists, who characteristically view themselves as the ones under attack—in this case, while they are oppressing others. The 2000 change is reminiscent of the first time the SBC changed the BFM in 1925 in response to the national debate over evolution. Then, at the height of the rise of fundamentalism, the SBC changed the BFM to express solidarity with creationist ideas. Seventy-five years later, the issue was gender roles, and the fundamentalist faction within the convention used power politics to enforce its views within the convention. This blatant use of power politics, however, violated their relationship with others who held opposing views. It also evidenced a complete closed-mindedness and absence of humility among convention leaders of the time. They would not even consider a dialogue with Southern Baptists who held other views.

These Southern Baptist Convention failures reveal important limits in their understanding of the gospel. First, the convention's racial dynamics expose white evangelical cultural tools working in concert with a transactional theology of salvation. The gender issue exposed more fully the absence of a commitment to relationship as the basis of the convention.

The delegates were incapable of respecting women as full human beings created in God's image within their community. The delegates' actions indicate that, for them, the most important thing in the kingdom is to be right and pure, not to create loving relationships. Within such an understanding of community life, a power move is completely justified. It keeps the body pure and right. And again, it cancels all need to be concerned with *process*, for only the end result matters.

Ironically, one of the three tools in the white cultural tool kit is relationalism. However, when relationalism is paired with the tool of individual freewill accountability, the limits of the SBC tool kit become clear. There is no tool to help Christians see that humanity, made in the divine image, has many distinctions and differences often used to subordinate and oppress people as a class of human beings and not as individuals. Relationships between different groups of people are insignificant, and people are unable to see the impact of history on individual attitudes and choices. Only relationships between individuals matter in understanding ethical choices. Relationships with women, and with the men who supported their equality in the Southern Baptist Convention, were ignored.

What, then, is needed? Reformation. The SBC needs a fundamental change in the tool kit by which it understands the world. To get there, however, the SBC will first need desire and humility. Then it will need to listen to the voices from the margins of its own convention. It might start with a deep study of one of the scripture texts it uses to defend its BFM position on the Church: "Do not lord [your leadership] over those in your charge, but be examples to the flock. . . . And all of you must clothe yourselves with humility in your dealings with one another, for 'God opposes the proud, but gives grace to the humble' " (1 Peter 5:3, 5b).

6

The Reconciliation Generation

It has been said that the gate of history turns on small hinges, and so do people's lives. The choices we make determine our destiny . . . some choices may seem more important than others, but no choice is insignificant.

—Thomas S. Monson

On December 28, 2000, twenty thousand future evangelical leaders heard a new voice call for a new kind of evangelicalism. In that moment, some believe, a spiritual deal was sealed. A worldview shifted, and the evangelical understanding of the good news would never be the same. That moment, however, was a hundred and twenty-three years in the making.

INTERVARSITY CHRISTIAN FELLOWSHIP ROOTS

InterVarsity began unofficially in 1877 when a group of Anglican students started a Bible study at the University of Cambridge, exactly one hundred years after Anglican William Wilberforce walked those grounds on his way to ending the British slave trade. Deep and broad social concern was at the core of the student movements of the late nineteenth century. However, in 1910, the evangelical split in the United States occurred also on British soil and affected InterVarsity. It went with the British fundamentalists, and InterVarsity Christian Fellowship became an official group in 1928 at the height of the fundamentalist revolt.[1] That year, the group sent its first missionary to North America. Canadian students had asked for help managing their rising movement. In response, Howard Guinness, a medical school graduate and vice-chair of the British movement, bought a one-way ticket to Canada to help fan the flames of a rising fundamentalist student movement. By 1937, Canada's Inter-Varsity was receiving requests from U.S. students to help plant ministries, and so, in 1938, they sent Stacy Woods, who would become the first secretary general of InterVarsity Christian Fellowship/USA.

Steven Hayner, former president of InterVarsity (1988–2001) and now professor of evangelism and church growth at Columbia Theological Seminary, reflected on the movement's history: "By the time InterVarsity reached the U.S., the threads of social justice were not really so important to the movement. By that point, InterVarsity was really only about basic discipleship: it was about Bible study, prayer, and evangelism on secular campuses."[2] Hayner emphasized that InterVarsity in the United States was founded by people from the Brethren denomination. The Church of the Brethren is a conservative Anabaptist/Pietist denomination that does not allow women to speak, much less preach or teach in church. Hence, InterVarsity/USA, like its British and Canadian predecessors, aligned with a fundamentalist movement.

"InterVarsity also had certain issues with the fundamentalist movement," Hayner added. "The fundamentalist movement overall was very anti-intellectual, but InterVarsity was working on college campuses." Ironically, it was InterVarsity's focus on careful and faithful study of scripture that led to dissonance within the fundamentalist movement. The dissonance revolved around two primary issues: gender and race.

INTERVARSITY'S DISSONANCE

When InterVarsity came to the United States in 1938, the European conflict that would become World War II was simmering. After Pearl Harbor in 1941, however, college men began to stream into the military from every sector of U.S. life, and women took over jobs typically reserved for men. InterVarsity was officially established in the United States a year later, in 1942. According to Hayner, the first four full-time InterVarsity staff members hired in the United States were women. Not only did women speak, they preached, taught, and developed Bible study curricula. In fact, within a year of the movement's establishment, staff member Jane Hollingsworth, based in New York City, introduced a new approach to Bible study. Rather than the fundamentalist prescriptive, a more exploratory, inductive approach to Bible study became InterVarsity's primary means of developing followers of Jesus. Two decades later, Barbara Boyd launched Bible & Life, a program that eventually involved over fifty thousand students and continues to this day.[3] Keith and Gladys Hunt remark on Stacy Woods's forward thinking in their book *For Christ and the University*: "His view of women in leadership was decades ahead of most other Christian leadership. Throughout the country, women staff workers were given the same assignments as men."[4]

Women in the workforce were not uncommon during the war, but once the men came home, many women lost their jobs. InterVarsity's practices remained unchanged despite the end of the war. Gwen Wong, InterVarsity's first full-time Asian American staff worker, pioneered the work in Hawaii in 1948. These practices stand in stark contrast to other campus-based evangelical ministries that had policies in place as late as the late 1990s that denied key leadership roles to women. If a male was present who could do the job, the woman would have to step down. Not so with InterVarsity.

InterVarsity's position on women in leadership has not been without conflict and cost. Steve Hayner was pressed to address the issue directly by writing a position paper on the subject. He noted:

> There were times when our behavior, as a covenantal fellowship with one another, began to be affected by individual commitments or views of women in leadership. For example: What happens if an area or region decides they want to invite a woman to be the biblical expositor at chapter camp? We had situations where individual chapters and individual staff would say we're not going to bring our students to this conference because you have a woman teaching.[5]

Hayner outlined two basic ways of approaching scripture legitimately on issues of women in leadership. He explained that the issue is an interpretive problem, not a problem with the Bible. One interpretive approach, Hayner said,

> takes the whole of scripture and interprets the parts vis-à-vis the whole. The whole of scripture is very af-

firming of women and their ministries. So the individual parts of scripture need to be interpreted in light of the whole. The other side says, "No, we interpret the whole in light of the individual parts. So, whatever the whole says, it cannot be contrary to all the little pieces."

Hayner concluded that InterVarsity, throughout its history, has used the first method and come down on the side of affirming women in their gifts and in any roles of leadership. Nothing in scripture, he noted, limits the roles of a woman with the appropriate gifts. Men must also be similarly gifted. In effect, InterVarsity said, "This is the way we're going to behave together. You can not believe it's true. You can be a part of churches that believe otherwise, but as long as you're going to live inside InterVarsity—inside this covenant fellowship, which you have elected to be a part of—this is the way we will serve together."[6]

InterVarsity fired a handful of staff who could not abide by the agreement. The greater cost, however, was the support of churches and denominations that had aligned with the movement historically but could not accept its stance on women in ministry. InterVarsity lost financial support due to its stance, but it was willing to pay that cost because of its conviction that this was the right thing to do.

Fourteen years before the Little Rock Nine desegregated Arkansas's Central High School and a decade before *Brown v. Topeka,* African American students in New York City became interested in InterVarsity. Jane Hollingsworth, who forged the way for inductive Bible study, forged a new path for InterVarsity. She began working with African American students on a historically black campus in the city.

At the time, all the InterVarsity students in the city gathered monthly at a board member's home. When Hollingsworth asked the board member if her black students could attend the gathering, she said "No." Hollingsworth, in her twenties at the time, took the matter to the board. She also had similar experiences when she tried to take her students to a YMCA near Atlantic City and again to a Christian conference center in New Jersey. InterVarsity was forced to make a choice. In the face of an inexorable tide of racist cultural norms, Stacy Woods "determined that InterVarsity would not hold any national conference at a site where people of other colors and backgrounds were excluded."[7] In June 1948, the board passed a three-point resolution:

(1) A Christian group in a Negro College shall be accepted without distinction as an InterVarsity Chapter,
(2) All national InterVarsity conferences shall be on a non-segregated basis,
(3) Since colored people relate segregation and the Christianity which we represent, we must demonstrate that in Christ there is neither black nor white.[8]

Hayner said that these policies created major tensions between InterVarsity and the fundamentalist movement. InterVarsity's original Doctrinal Basis of Faith was crafted in response to fundamentalists who looked at Woods's stance on women in leadership and racial integration and insisted. "You're not really Bible-believing Christians."[9] Woods shot back, "We most certainly are." Woods then crafted InterVarsity's first Doctrinal Basis of Faith using the fundamentalist movement's creed, the Five Fundamentals of Faith, to verify the integrity of InterVarsity's work to those churches.[10] However, says Hayner, "The tension that has always been a part of InterVarsity is when you actually study the scriptures, and not just the doctrine derived from the scriptures; one of the things you very quickly realize is that the scriptures care for more than what our narrow doctrine states." Mimi Haddad, president of Christians for Biblical Equality, explains:

> Renewal and spiritual awakening for evangelicals comes through an engagement with the text—the Bible, where people of faith encounter God's Spirit working in the text. We encounter the very living presence of God in that text with a sense of humility—with a sense of wanting to learn, and a desire to be renewed, and a willingness to confess that we need to put self-interest aside for the purpose of the mission of the church in this broken world. Justice is holiness and that's what happens in renewal movements as Christians realize there are all these places where we've been dead-wrong.[11]

Just a few years after Hollingsworth won the day and two years before *Brown v. Topeka*, Ivery Harvey, a student nearing graduation at Wayne State University in Detroit, Michigan, wanted to pioneer full-time black campus ministry in the Southeast. InterVarsity had hired one part-time black staff member, Eugene Callander, who served from 1947–1949, but up to that point, it had no full-time black staff. With Harvey, the board of trustees faced a new crossroads: Would InterVarsity make a clear break with the theologically indoctrinated fundamentalist norm of racialized segregation and hire an African American staff on a full-time basis? Much debate over the decision reached down into the ranks of cam-

pus staff. In the end, "each InterVarsity staff said they would
tender their resignations if a Negro staff did not have 'the
same status as the rest of us.' "[12]

LIVING IN THE TENSION OF BOTH/AND

InterVarsity's history raises an important question: "How
could a U.S. movement born in the soil of Calvinist fundamentalism produce these kinds of progressive choices in the
areas of gender and race?" The twentieth century's fundamentalism, from which U.S. InterVarsity sprang, was a
reaction *against* the progressive social gospel. Yet its accep-
tance of the authority of the text paired with an inductive
model of interpreting it led InterVarsity to value things that
others, who said they were Bible-believing, could not accept.

A key foundation of the InterVarsity student movement
in England was its Anglican theological heritage. Ron Benefiel, president of the Nazarene Theological Seminary and a
Wesleyan scholar, explained important features of the Anglican tradition in a recent interview: "Anglicanism represents a
middle way (*via media*) between the Catholic and Protestant
traditions," he said. Its theology, liturgy, and church practices
were developed by the Church of England, which had roots
in indigenous Celtic Christianity and Catholic liturgical
structures. The Anglican Church was established during the
Protestant Reformation, but its roots reach as far back as the
thirteenth century when *ecclesia anglicana*, a Medieval Latin
phrase, was used to refer to the English Church. Benefiel explained that Anglicanism tends to take a *both/and* approach
to faith life, the way Catholics use scripture, tradition, and
ritual equally. In the Anglican view, the gospel begins in Genesis and ends in Revelation. It traces the dynamic story of

God's pursuit to restore right relationships with humanity and all of creation. That pursuit includes the redemption of the broken relationships between humanity and the rest of God's creation as well. At its core Anglican theology is incarnational, believing spirit and flesh are joined together in creation; and dynamic, viewing historical change as an arena of divine transformation.[13] And, according to Rev. Paula Harris, rector of the Episcopal Church of the Resurrection in Wisconsin, its threefold conception of authority, which includes scripture, tradition, and reason, works in combination with the gospel to create a dynamic faith that holds many things in tension.[14]

The Anglican Church saw the rise of two major early movements. The seventeenth-century Cambridge Platonists emphasized idealist reason and the universal rationality of the faith found in intelligible forms that went beyond sense perception and individual personal experience. Revivals led by John Wesley and Charles Simeon reemphasized the importance of individual faith and the personal experience of the Holy Spirit, as well as social engagement.[15] It was this Wesleyan revival movement that gave birth to InterVarsity and influenced both its emphasis on personal piety and its social engagement.

As InterVarsity invited people of color into its ranks, it was pressed to draw from its Anglican roots as it faced challenges to its own sense of truth and reality—narratives from those "with their backs against the wall," as Howard Thurman put it. A fundamentalist, modern paradigm would have inhibited InterVarsity's ability to integrate the histories of people of color. The modern industrial age—the age of imperialism and colonization—is characterized by the domination of one power over another, one sense of reality over another; it was an either/or age in which Europeans and white Americans imposed their own ideas of "universal" Enlightenment truths, limited by their cultures, on the vast peoples and cultures of Africa, Asia, and Latin America. Colonizers set up walls of difference between the "enlightened" truths of their own group and the "backward" or "primitive" others they segregated themselves from, oppressed, and, in some cases, annihilated as contaminants. Thus, in the fundamentalist worldview—a product of the modern age—to accept the narratives of the other as true meant one's own truth was false. InterVarsity may have pushed its way to life through modern fundamentalist soil, but its hybrid foundations enabled the organization to confront the colonial spirit within its own DNA, evidence of an openness still uncommon in fundamentalist organizations.

In December 1967, eight months after Martin Luther King Jr. gave his controversial speech, "Beyond Vietnam: A Time to Break Silence," at the Riverside Church in New York City, none of the nine thousand students attending InterVarsity's Urbana missions convention knew that King would be dead within four months. At the conference Evan Adams, a former InterVarsity staff member, took the stage and spoke to the students about the times in which they lived: "Youth are struggling today, as you know well, to find out from themselves and their adults, 'What's real?' To youth in the present generation, we give either packages or institutions or quick answers, but youth are still asking, 'What's real?' " In his talk, Adams said the world was undergoing a "great transition." He said they were "moving from the past to the future." After talking about the failed way the church had addressed the question of Vietnam, Adams ended his speech with a call: "Today youth are questioning our institutions. They're asking us if we can prove, if we can pass on, and if we can grant to them the privileges of the future. I'm convinced that the future lies in youth; it always has. And we give it to you in this convention."[16]

Two hundred black students were sitting in the audience when Adams offered them the future. A group of those students were moved by his invitation. In response, they spent the entire night in prayer.[17] In the morning they approached a group of InterVarsity leaders to present a petition with demands that called for changes the movement would have to make if it was going to reach black students.

InterVarsity stood at a crossroads, again. Would this evangelical organization, with Anglican roots and a fundamentalist heritage, listen to those with their backs against the wall or would they let their petition fall on deaf ears? Neil Rendall and Pete Hammond, two white staff members, were present at this meeting and admit the leaders were scared.[18] Nonetheless, they listened.

As a result, InterVarsity's president at the time, John Alexander, called a meeting with black student leaders Carl Ellis, Elward Ellis, and Bill Bentley after the conference. They discussed the issues the petition raised. They formed the Urbana Student Advisory Committee. InterVarsity created a promotional film to recruit black students to attend Urbana 1970, and accepted the black students' recommendation that Tom Skinner speak at it.

Skinner stood on the stage at Urbana 1970 in front of 12,304 students. This time, seven hundred were black. Skinner called the InterVarsity movement to grab hold of a *both/and* gospel: he urged the students to seek justice as a primary way God works in the world; to perceive the good news as being tied to the redemption of all relationships, not just the relationship of the individual to God; and to retrieve a vision of God's kingdom, where peace and wholeness for all humanity and all creation would be restored. The gathering tried to listen to this voice from the margins. InterVarsity stood in the tension between the modern and the postcolonial age for another twenty years.

Over those two decades, the organization wrestled with itself. Sometimes its fears were strongest; other times its best visions prevailed to push it into an ungraspable future. As vision won out over fear, leaders from the white evangelical ranks of InterVarsity, like Ron Sider, began to take up Skinner's struggle with books like *Rich Christians in an Age of Hunger* (1977). Skinner's allies called InterVarsity and the larger evangelical church to expand their understanding of the good news and to reembrace a worldview shaped by the kingdom of God. The movement continued to invite people of color to the table. John Perkins joined InterVarsity's board of directors in the 1980s. By 1985, Gordon MacDonald, InterVarsity's new president, assembled a Multiethnic Task Force of a dozen senior staff to answer two questions: (1) What would InterVarsity look like if it became a true multiethnic ministry? and (2) What structural changes would be necessary if this could be accomplished?[19]

In our interview, Steve Hayner said that when he became president of InterVarsity, the first thing that faced him was a report from the Multiethnic Task Force. He knew that to make racial reconciliation a major value, the organization would need to bring its behavior and decision making into line with that value:

You can hold a value, but if you don't align with a value, that value will never have any traction. In order to do that we're going to have to change how InterVarsity is led. We're going to have to ensure that people of color are included in the decision making at every level. We're going to have to make a major effort at recruiting and developing staff of color. But most importantly, the report underlined again something InterVarsity had long believed, but had not really acted on—the kingdom of God is a multiethnic reality. So, if InterVarsity wants to be a movement that follows God's heart with a biblical worldview, we will need to have a multiethnic worldview.[20]

Hayner worked with the new Multiethnic Ministries Department, headed by Samuel Barkat, to make multiethnicity one of InterVarsity's top three national values throughout the 1990s. They addressed the issue on every level of the organization: beginning with staff training institutes, they developed theological foundations for the value and began to publish Bible study guides to address it. Hayner spent huge amounts of time throughout his presidency transfusing the value for multiethnicity into the bloodstream of the movement.

InterVarsity is not a movement that runs on hierarchical authority. It has always been and still is a grassroots movement. Hayner could not simply issue a decree and have his word "be so" throughout the movement. Consequently, he and the multiethnic team had to figure out ways to influence staff on the ground. A series of events that pushed race relations to the forefront of the national conscience moved the InterVarsity national movement forward:

- 1991: The videotaped police beating of Rodney King and the verdict which exonerated the police of all charges were followed by the Los Angeles riots.
- 1991: A Korean storeowner in Los Angeles shot and killed fifteen-year-old Latasha Harlins.
- 1994: The anti-immigrant Proposition 187 passed in California.
- 1995: The O.J. Simpson trial resulted in a controversial verdict that evoked divergent responses along racial lines.
- 1995: The Promise Keepers began their racial reconciliation movement.
- 1996: In California anti–affirmative action Proposition 209 passed.
- 1999: Four New York police officers fired forty-one times at point-blank range into the body of an unarmed twenty-five-year-old Guinean immigrant, Amadou Diallo, hitting him nineteen times, and were exonerated of any wrongdoing.
- 1999: In a racially motivated shooting rampage in Chicago, the former Northwestern University basketball coach, African American Ricky Birdsong, and a Korean graduate student, Won-Soon Yun, were killed and several others were wounded.
- 1999: African American James Byrd was beaten, decapitated, and dragged through the streets of Jasper, Texas.

These and many other tragedies touched InterVarsity deeply. As a result, grassroots initiatives took shape within InterVarsity communities on campuses throughout the country. In Greater Los Angeles, I worked with Doug and Sandy Schaupp and Tracey Gee to develop a dialogue structure called "Race Matters" that we eventually renamed "Family Time." It gave multiethnic InterVarsity chapters ways to engage the issues within their communities through dialogue. Orlando Crespo, then New York City area director, developed a racism simulation exercise he enacted for all New York students at year-end leadership training camps. Chicago staff focused on strong training for their ethnic-specific chapters to build positive ethnic identities. This strategy was designed to increase the effectiveness of interethnic reconciliation efforts. These models began to catch on, and as they did, the value of racial reconciliation permeated the movement from the top down and from the bottom up.

InterVarsity had previously begun summer projects in the mid-1970s in New York City, inspired by John Perkins's Summer Project model. They multiplied in the 1990s as staff began to understand the value of short-term displacement experiences in the development of their student leaders. Staff experienced what Emerson and Smith discovered through analysis: immersion experiences are necessary for evangelicals to be challenged and stretched to include a multiethnic perspective. Guided by National Urban Project Director Randy White, author of *Journey to the Center of the City*, Kevin Blue led the Los Angeles Urban Project, Brenda Salter McNeil and John Hochovar led the Chicago Urban Project, Orlando Crespo led the New York Urban Project, and scores more sprang up all over the country. Each offered deep transformative experiences that challenged and stretched the worldviews of hundreds of students who would eventually leave the campus to lead the church and change the world.

Then came Urbana 2000.

Nearly all of InterVarsity staff, thousands of InterVarsity students, hundreds of interdenominational church groups, and scores of mission agencies attended the Urbana missions convention every three years; 20,241 attended Urbana 2000. The Urbana conventions are InterVarsity's best opportunities to influence its staff, student leaders, and the general church through the best teaching available in the evangelical world. In 2000 the official theme was worship, but racial reconciliation permeated the entire conference. According to Paula Harris, who was the program director for the Urbana conference, the idea was that "we cannot worship God well if we are in enmity with each other."[21]

One hundred and twenty-three years after InterVarsity's inception, African American Brenda Salter McNeil, former InterVarsity staff member and president of the Chicago-based Overflow Ministries, took the stage during the evening session of the first full day. She started with the words, "It was July 2, 1999. I'll never forget it," and shared her personal experience dealing with the death of Ricky Birdsong, a personal church friend. Ricky's racially motivated death rocked her soul. It caused her to hate the hater who shot her friend—right in front of his children. It caused her to question the faithfulness and goodness of God. It caused this racial reconciler to scorn the thought of reconciliation.[22]

Salter McNeil shared how, in the midst of her questioning, she was struck by the words of Isaiah 6: "Woe is me! I am lost, for I am a person of unclean lips, and I live among a people of unclean lips." She realized that like Isaiah, she too was a person of unclean lips and her entire generation was a people of unclean lips. She was shaken when she sensed God saying to her: "The very same thing that was in the heart of that guy that killed Ricky is in all of your hearts." Then she confessed her fear of the other and her apathy toward the other's plight. She mentioned "an awesome text" that had just come out called *Divided by Faith*. She rebuked the apathy of her generation:

> Basically the writers of that text have come to believe that the church is comfortable in its isolationism, and we don't care that we don't care! And that's why we don't do anything. And that's why we don't try to change. And that's why we cry out more about things like homosexuality or abortion, and we won't say a thing about racism because we don't care. We don't care. It doesn't bug us that much. It doesn't affect us, it doesn't hurt us. We are safe, or so we think.[23]

Salter McNeil ended her talk by being the first to confess: "Hey, God, I'm sorry. You're right. My heart's messed up. And Ricky, I swear I didn't know I had anything to do with it. But I'm really, really sorry."

I was Salter McNeil's personal assistant at Urbana 2000. I remember how uneasy she was that night as she left the stage. Salter McNeil, who comes from a Pentecostal background and is known for her powerful prayers, felt like there was more that was supposed to happen, but she did not know what.

The Asian American community was abuzz immediately after Salter McNeil spoke. They noticed that she had focused exclusively on the death of the black man and had failed to even mention the Korean person who also died in the Chicago shooting rampage. By omitting Won-Soon Yu from the story, they explained, Salter McNeil had dishonored Yu in death.

At the end of the morning session on the second day, Brenda Salter McNeil mounted the stage again. She had asked the convention leaders for time to go back onstage to apologize and they gave her two minutes. Two minutes may seem like nothing, but stage time is the most valued commodity at Urbana conventions. It was significant. Salter McNeil, a woman of great pride and presence, took the stage weak and vulnerable. Salter McNeil, a woman who specialized in racial reconciliation in Chicago where an entrenched black/white binary reinforced the popular perception that only whites could be racist, opened her mouth to speak and was broken. Salter McNeil, a woman who helped lead InterVarsity's national movement forward into racial reconciliation at a time when InterVarsity staff were deeply divided over the question of whether people of color could be racist in the United States given their lack of power, asked for forgiveness. She confessed, agreeing with her Asian and Asian American brothers and sisters, that she misused her platform power with the omission of Won-Soon Yu's story from her story. She agreed that she had indeed dishonored Won-Soon Yu. She also confessed that she now understood what it must feel like to be white and feel like all your best efforts lead to humbling moments of failure.

Even now, it is difficult to understand why this moment had such profound impact. Just the night before, Salter McNeil had confessed in general terms that the fear and apathy in the racist shooter's heart was also in her own. Yet, on the next morning, general allusions to racism gave way to concrete confessions as Salter McNeil identified partiality in her own heart, made manifest in the act of exclusion. In that moment, InterVarsity was confronted with the complexity of racial dynamics in an increasingly multiethnic society. As a result, it was the first time in this generation that a national InterVarsity figure made it plain: racism, or the concept's biblical corollary, racial "partiality" (Acts 10), is a part of the human condition, not just a white problem. Salter McNeil describes the moment in her book *A Credible Witness: Reflections on Power, Evangelism and Race*:

> There was an immediate reaction throughout the assembly hall. The worship leader standing on stage began to cry. One woman told me that she watched the service on closed-circuit television in her hotel room and when she heard those words she gasped and began to weep.[24]

Salter McNeil then strayed from her planned statement. The memory of the next moment reverberates in the lives of those who were there. She looked out over the assembly of twenty thousand and addressed this emerging generation. She talked of how previous generations had tried to reach the promised land of racial reconciliation in the United States, but never made it. She said she believed this generation would be the reconciliation generation. Then Salter McNeil called all those who wanted to be a part of the reconciliation generation to stand where they were. The assembly stood. Steven Hayner remembers that moment well:

> I was thinking, this is really the clarion call to a new kind of evangelicalism. Because, not only was multiethnicity a part of the agenda, but back at Urbana '90, we identified other issues we thought were really important that were not typical evangelical issues, like the environment and economic

justice, and focused on them throughout the entire Urbana.[25]

In 1990, InterVarsity Press published a Bible study series that gave biblical foundations for Christian involvement in several justice issues. The studies were used at the 1990 Urbana conference. Paula Harris remembers: "We had a huge emphasis on justice at that convention and actually put on ten or fifteen tracks about major justice issues complete with Bible studies. Glandion Carney and Mary Fisher ran that program."[26] Harris points out that there are still fundamentalists angry about that Urbana program. One online fundamentalist rant accused the program of being New Age, liberal, ecumenical, and heretical.[27]

Hayner was also a founding member of the Evangelical Environmental Network, created in 1989. It was the first large-scale move by evangelicals to address issues of the environment. "So, by the time we got to 2000," Hayner explained,

it was like the yeast had begun to leaven the loaf. We begin to see this whole idea of the justice generation—the idea that this will be a generation that will begin to take some new steps forward, not only in the area of multiethnicity, but in a whole host of kingdom issues.[28]

Two nights later, after Salter McNeil made her apology and call, Gary Haugen, InterVarsity alumnus and founder of the International Justice Mission (IJM), took the stage. He spoke from a legal, human-rights framework, not just on general "justice." He spoke of the ways IJM is leveraging international and local laws to protect and preserve the image of God in human beings around the world. The United Nations and international law were usually held suspect in evangelical settings as forces competing with the kingdom of God. This was the first time I ever heard an evangelical speak of international human-rights work as a partner of the gospel. Those at Urbana 2000 lacked the language yet to understand what they were witnessing, but in this moment they knew they were indeed entering the future.

"Your Kingdom Come, Your Will Be Done" was the theme of Urbana 2003. InterVarsity leaders pushed the edges of evangelicalism again. Program director Paula Harris invited Ray Aldred to address evangelical America. Aldred, director of the First Nations Alliance Churches of Canada (Cree Nation), stood at the podium and read his message. There were no sweeping dips or falls of inflection. There were no grand displays of emotion—only postcolonial words to postmodern evangelicals—an offering. More than nineteen thousand evangelicals could barely breathe for the thickness of the moment, as Aldred read from his notes:

> As you begin to reach out beyond your own boundaries, as you choose to love the other people, as you chose to make yourself vulnerable, as you begin to try and communicate the gospel in the heart language of other people, you realize that *your* world, *your* construct of reality is too small. You realize that to communicate in another heart language you must speak from your heart and live out your spirituality on the level of human suffering. You realize that your presentation and your words are not enough. They are limited. You begin to understand that you are out

there trying to convert the lost but you are still in need of conversion and re-creation. And you begin to hear the gospel story again.[29]

It was true. InterVarsity was in the midst of relearning the gospel. Four spiritual laws could not contain this good news. Laws were too small and the news too big. This was news of redemption and restoration, of redeemed relationships and restored peace . . . a peace scripture says humanity experienced once long before the break, the crash, the tragedy of the Fall.

That night Jonathan Maracle & Broken Walls, a First Nations band with drum circle and dancers, led nineteen thousand sons and daughters who had inherited the benefits and tragedies of colonialism in a friendship dance. For a moment, all were living in the circle of shalom. A piece of something had been restored, for a moment.

MOVING PAST SHADOWS

Over the past two decades, five major influences converged in InterVarsity to create a great shift in what staff and students perceive as the good news. The movement's faith legacy, its national work on the issues of multiethnicity and women in leadership, its grassroots work in the value and practice of racial reconciliation, the Urbana conventions, and Urban Projects have all played a role in broadening the historically white evangelical worldviews of its staff and members. This shift is best illustrated by the movement's current work to share the good news on campus.

Scott McLane, InterVarsity staff worker in Los Angeles, began his tenure at predominantly white Occidental College as part of a mostly white team. When McLane first joined the staff, evangelism was shaped by the Willow Creek Church bridge model that highlighted the "God-shaped void" in individuals' souls. The model proposed that all are created for God, feel that nature as a longing, and try to fill it with other things. Nothing, however, can fill a soul's thirst for God except God. "That was the main mode of operation—trying to help people move toward God, through personal satisfaction."[30] InterVarsity also used a method called Groups Investing God (GIGs) to move interested students toward personal fulfillment through a relationship with Jesus. This model did not necessarily encompass evangelism (sharing the good news) that also included systemic reconciliation.

McLane eventually moved to East Los Angeles to plant an InterVarsity chapter at Cal State University, Los Angeles. In East L.A. McLane was immersed in a mostly Latino community. At Cal State L.A., he was guiding a mostly black chapter. These assignments displaced McLane and immersed him in the world of the others. In discussing his earlier experiences of evangelism in InterVarsity, McLane explained,

> I didn't throw that away, but the students that I'm meeting have limited time because they're working twenty to forty hours per week plus going to school and trying to help their families out. So, do I do a GIG with them and approach their need in that mode of evangelism? Or do I start a study group for them, so they can write a paper and pass their freshmen English class and stay in college? Does that count as good news? And where does Jesus enter into that? Am I just sort of doing good for them, but

not really helping them interact with Jesus? Or is
that also helping them to interact with Jesus and thus
also a part of evangelism?[31]

Through his experiences, McLane moved from an either/
or understanding of evangelism to a both/and approach,
reminiscent of John Perkins's both/and model developed in Mendenhall, Mississippi. Displacement reshaped
McLane's view of the gospel. Now he considers ministry to
the felt needs of whole persons and their communities *as*
evangelism.

InterVarsity's evangelism around the nation has taken off
over the past two years. Alec Hill, InterVarsity president
since 2001, explained in a 2007 interview that African American InterVarsity evangelism specialist York Moore has been
organizing evangelism events in places such as Clarion, a
state school in Pennsylvania, UCLA, Ohio State, and Michigan: "We have seen anywhere between fifty and seventy students becoming believers in a week."[32] These events
combine three elements: first, social justice has focused on
sex slavery through partnership with International Justice
Mission or on the AIDS pandemic through partnership with
World Vision; second, the arts are incorporated through the
use of collage, sculpture, and music to tap into students'
emotional response to the issue; and third, each event includes the proclamation of the gospel. "We're seeing students coming to the Lord," Hill says, "like we just haven't
seen. The last two years we've seen more new believers than
we have seen ever in the history of InterVarsity."[33]

InterVarsity's impact on the worldview shift within the
larger evangelical world is debatable. If counted by numbers,
the impact is modest at best. InterVarsity reaches approxi-

mately thirty-thousand students each year. Only a quarter of the Urbana missions convention participants are InterVarsity students, and each year, only 1,500 InterVarsity students participate in Urban Projects.[34] Those are the numbers. However, the impact can also be measured by the influence of leaders. Gary Haugen, founder and president of International Justice Mission is an InterVarsity alumnus. Ruth Lewis Bentley, National Black Evangelical Association (NBEA) treasurer and director of administration, is an InterVarsity alumna. Andy Crouch, editor of *Christianity Today's* Christian Vision Project is an InterVarsity alumnus. Luis Cortés Jr., president of Esperanza USA, a Latino lobbying agency, is an alumnus of InterVarsity's New York Urban Project.[35] Jeff White, pastor of New Song Church—a prophetic interracial community working toward economic justice in the heart of Harlem; Brenda Salter McNeil, author and racial reconciliation specialist; Mac Pier, executive director of Concerts of Prayer–New York; Lisa and Derek Engdahl, co-executive directors of Servant Partners; and Mark Earley, president and CEO of Prison Fellowship Ministries, are all InterVarsity alumni/ae. Ron Sider, president of Evangelicals for Social Concern, and Bill Pannell, influential black evangelical theologian are InterVarsity alumni. Carl Ellis, director of Project Joseph, is an InterVarsity alumnus. Samuel Escobar served as general secretary of InterVarsity Christian Fellowship–Canada (1972–1975), and Carlos Rene Padilla served the International Evangelical Fellowship of Students (IFES) as associate general secretary for Latin America (InterVarsity was a founder of IFES). And John Stott led the way, along with Padilla, Escobar, and a host of other InterVarsity staff in the 1970s to press for the Lausanne Covenant of 1974, which included a call for social and international justice for all evangelicals. Stott came out of InterVarsity's Anglican parent-student movement at the University of Cambridge.

In addition to these established leaders, there is a new generation of InterVarsity alumni/ae leading urban centers across the country. Thousands of alumni/ae who participated in Urban Projects, Urbana conventions, and campus chapters have put the Three Rs to work. They have moved into urban centers to teach in underserved schools, advocate for economic and environmental justice, start theater companies for at-risk youth, and live as multiethnic witnessing communities in blighted urban neighborhoods.

These leaders probably caught the vision of the kingdom of God while practicing Jane Hollingsworth's inductive Bible study method. Or maybe they were on a summer project at John Perkins's Voice of Calvary Ministries. Or perhaps it was the moment they stood in response to Brenda Salter Mc-Neil's call for a new kind of evangelicalism. In any case, they are still standing. And they are bearing witness.

InterVarsity Christian Fellowship has been and is an important influence on the evangelical shift happening today. InterVarsity's story demonstrates a transformative journey that created new routes for Christians to follow Jesus. That journey came mostly as a result of a covenantal fellowship of diverse staff and students working out how they would live life together on the same mission field—the campus. While InterVarsity's journey is unique, the fact that the organization experienced a worldview shift is not.

Campus Crusade is currently in the midst of a major shift of its own. It was born out of InterVarsity in 1951 on the campus of UCLA. Bill Bright was an InterVarsity student who was disturbed by the lack of evangelism on campus. He sought "the lost." Bright broke off from InterVarsity and formed Campus Crusade for Christ with a primary mission to seek and save the lost on college campuses. Since then, Campus Crusade has grown into an international multidimensional ministry. According to Phil Stump, human resources director, most Campus Crusade staff come from Reformed and Calvinist evangelical backgrounds; most come on staff directly from conservative and historically fundamentalist seminaries, including Dallas Theological Seminary, Westminster Theological Seminary; and Reformed Theological Seminary.[36]

I was involved with Campus Crusade throughout my years as an undergraduate student at Rutgers University and almost joined their staff team. I learned the Four Spiritual Laws inside and out.[37] I knew them so well, my friends and I would make up songs using the laws as lyrics to poke fun at that little gold booklet, so central to life in Campus Crusade. Campus Crusade used the Four Spiritual Laws to communicate the gospel into the new millennium. But something happened that challenged the organization's simple, legalistic framework of the good news: Hurricane Katrina.

Ted Gandy, national director of Campus Crusade's urban project ministry, Here's Life Inner City, says:

> Campus Crusade as a whole is having a real shift in campus ministry because of Katrina. They thought they'd send a couple thousand students down to observe. . . . I think to date they've sent seventeen thousand. That's ten times what they expected to send, and I think that in the process they've understood how good works fit into the gospel, and that we

can't separate out the good news from our good works.[38]

Until the Katrina disaster, Campus Crusade's perception of the gospel fit classic fundamentalist theology, Dallas Willard's bar-code faith. Thus, in Campus Crusade's conception, to be saved, all a sinner had to do was pray the sinner's prayer, which confessed the need for Jesus's death on the cross to pay the penalty for his sins and the sinner would be saved. Bar-code faith is about cognitive belief. Willard railed against this conception of faith, pointing out that in biblical times the concept of faith was not passive. It was active. It was not about assent to some ideas. It was about belief demonstrated through action.[39]

Hurricane Katrina has catalyzed a monumental shift in the Campus Crusade conception of the gospel. Their new conception of faith cannot be divorced from works. With such a shift, the early-twentieth-century split between fundamentalists and the social gospel—the Scofield/Rauschenbusch divorce—may be ending. If Candy's observations hold, we are witnessing the reconciliation of two church factions who claimed irreconcilable differences just a century ago. Gandy believes the evangelical church is headed in just that direction:

I see this type of shift happening now not just in Campus Crusade but among evangelicals as a whole. The attempt to keep the gospel pure, which of course started in the previous century—separating out the social gospel from the spiritual gospel—that whole conversation has ended. There's really very much of a coming back together of both the Great Commission and the Great Commandment,[40] and this separation that was so unnatural, it seems to me, has ended. . . . There's just an assumption, literally across the board among evangelicals, that we need to be actively caring for marginalized people and serving "the least of these."[41]

It appears evangelicals have passed from one century to the next. It seems they left dysfunctional division behind. They are discovering again a *both/and* gospel.

Emerson and Smith's theory of the effects of white evangelicals' immersion into networks of color has played itself out in the transformation of InterVarsity Christian Fellowship and is beginning to make its impact in the transformation of Campus Crusade for Christ. Within both white evangelical movements, the white evangelical worldview was challenged and stretched as the movements increased the presence and influence of people of color within the community. In InterVarsity's case this transformation occurred over the course of a century. Campus Crusade staff and students have been jarred to change through their post-Katrina experience in New Orleans. They are gaining new cultural tools as they immerse themselves in devastated communities of color affected by the catastrophe. The previously entrenched poverty and marginalization revealed through the storm is dislodging the organizations' bar-code conception of faith. A new generation is coming to believe the *good news* must be good news to all—especially to those with their backs against the wall.

7

Good News . . . Again!

The Bible clearly states that God has favorites and his fa-
vorites are the poor. There are more than two thousand
verses on the poor in scripture. To ignore them is not only
to be ignorant, it is to be disobedient.[1]

—Rick Warren, senior pastor, Saddleback Church

When I asked fifty-five of the sixty-seven evangelical leaders I interviewed if they believed that evangelical perceptions of the gospel are expanding, virtually all of them said, "Yes." The evangelical worldview is expanding beyond an individualistic, static, legal conception of the cross and the resurrection of Jesus—one that believes Jesus came solely to pay the penalty for the individual's sin. The evangelical understanding of the cross and resurrection is beginning to include the dynamic restoration of every relationship broken by the Fall in Genesis 3. In this dynamic view, Jesus came to restore humanity's relationship with God, but he also came to restore humans' relationships with each other, with systems, with the rest of creation, and even individuals' relationships with themselves, as well as relationships between nations. Evangelical leaders—in states like Texas, Missouri, and Kansas as well as in Boston, Los Angeles, New York, and

Chicago—said, yes, this change is happening, and, at its heart, it is the coming of the kingdom of God and shalom.

Kingdom of God theology is not new. It was the driving force behind the Protestant social movements of the late nineteenth century. It was reintroduced to evangelical America in the twentieth century through the teachings of Thurman and King, among others, and gained a greater audience through the work of evangelicals like Perkins, Skinner, Sider, Campolo, and Wallis. In both the nineteenth century and second half of the twentieth century, kingdom theology was paired with the doctrine of perfectionism, the belief that salvation begins with the individual's transformation in the journey toward Christlikeness, but it does not stop there. It moves out and seeks to transform the entire world as God established his rule on earth through Christ.

Iva E. Carruthers, general secretary of the Samuel DeWitt Proctor Conference, a black church leadership development network, reminded me in our interview that kingdom of God theology in the hands of the Religious Right was corrupted. It sought cultural hegemony.[2] In *Blow the Trumpet in Zion*, Carruthers warns,

> The kingdom theology, also called "Dominion theology," has a major proponent in Bishop Earl Paulk, a conservative evangelical pastor from Atlanta, who has said, "Kingdom theology is a whole new theology. . . . What we're doing is setting up a network by which we can spread propaganda . . . so that the systems of the world will collapse because of their inability to survive, and what will be left will be a system the church has built." This agenda is to create

a "Christian culture that will have dominion over the world."[3]

This understanding of kingdom theology is born of the fundamentalist salvation theology that reduces the doctrine of perfectionism to individual moral purity. The purpose of Jesus in establishing the kingdom of God, according to this theology, is to "perfect" the world spiritually. This understanding of God's kingdom misses the mark because of two missteps in its construction: (1) it conceives of "perfection" with a dualistic Greek worldview that splits spirit and flesh, whereas the Jews of Jesus's day understood "perfection" through a mixed Hebrew and Greek paradigm that tended to integrate spirit and flesh; and (2) its approach to scripture discounts the bulk of biblical counsel, which concerns itself with the material, worldly conditions of the poor, the marginalized, and the vulnerable as a dimension of faith in God.

Aristotle defined perfection in an object as "that which is complete, that which is good and that which has attained its purpose."[4] "Perfection" in the Hebrew mind-set did not focus on the object of perception. It was not an individualistic concept. It, like the Hebrew culture, was focused on communal life. Thus, to be perfect in the Hebrew mind-set was to love God, love justice, and love neighbors perfectly.

For example, Jesus called his disciples to perfection when he gave his most famous sermon—the Sermon on the Mount. In Matthew 5:44 Jesus called his disciples to "love their enemies so that they could be children of their Father in heaven." Next he gave them the charge that established the doctrine of perfectionism: "Be perfect, therefore, as your heavenly Father is perfect." Jesus links perfection with how one loves. To be perfect is to love perfectly. To love perfectly is to love everyone, even one's enemies.

Kingdom theology paired with shalom theology corrects Paulk's view of the kingdom of God. Shalom theology is rooted in a relational framework and in the book of Genesis. Salvation is the restoration of one's relationship with God and all the relationships in creation, broken in the Fall. To spread the reign of God is to restore all relationships on earth. Thus, shalom necessarily connects the individual's well-being with the well-being of every human being and with the whole of creation. To live perfectly on earth is to love perfectly.

In the early to mid-1990s the theology of shalom began to emerge in evangelical theological circles. It usually takes a decade for major theological concepts to make their way from the classroom to the pulpit. That would place the breakthrough of shalom theology in evangelical circles be-tween 2000–2005. I was taught the concept in 2003 as it began to make its way into InterVarsity Christian Fellowship.

What's more, recent work by Miroslav Volf, professor of theology at Yale Divinity School, attempts to recover the lost foundations of Martin Luther's doctrine of justification. Volf explains in *Free of Charge* that Luther

> is known for his rediscovery of God's justification of the ungodly. Instead of condemning sinners, God, rich in mercy, bestows righteousness upon sinners, justifying them irrespective of their merits or de-merits. At the heart of this justification of the un-godly is God's generous love. As both creator and redeemer, God is a pure giver.[5]

Thus, Volf explains, even Luther, the inspiration behind Calvin's legal paradigm of salvation, saw justification as an act of love prompted by God's desire for a relationship with his creation.

LUKE 4:18–19: THE INAUGURAL ADDRESS

Christian Churches Together in the USA is a growing forum of denominational and organizational leaders representing five "faith families" within Christendom. These families include historic Protestant denominations and the Roman Catholic and Orthodox churches, as well as Racial Ethnic and Evangelical/Pentecostal churches. The leaders began meeting informally in September 2001 and incorporated in 2007. At the 2007 annual meeting, the five families agreed they would focus on two things—poverty and evangelism. Steve Haas, vice president of World Vision, explained in a recent interview what happened next: "Assignments were made to various members of the five families to speak about poverty and evangelism. The majority of those who were asked, independent of one another, decided to focus on Luke 4." That included the evangelicals. Haas continued, "In doing so, they underlined the fact that release from poverty and evangelism are indispensable partners in the mission of the good news—that, in fact, they *are* the good news."[6] In addition, when I asked my interviewees, "What do you consider to be the good news of Christianity?" most said, "The coming of the kingdom of God," or they referenced Luke 4:18–19.

This understanding of the good news has not been prevalent in evangelical America since the nineteenth century. If I had asked the same leaders that question only a decade ago, their answers likely would have focused exclusively on how God can meet the individual's needs for fulfillment. Fifteen years ago, some might have mentioned John 3:16 or the Four Spiritual Laws. The focus on Luke 4 is a departure from the most prevalent twentieth-century evangelical conceptions of the gospel.

Currently, evangelical theologians and others are working out new biblically grounded conceptions of the kingdom of God and shalom in classrooms and theological conferences. Their theological work will find the light of day in church pulpits and pews within a decade. For the time being, though, these leaders' responses are a signal that a paradigm of the kingdom of God linked with an evangelical conception of shalom is gaining traction. This link is altering the evangelical worldview and loosening the death grip of the Religious Right's agenda on the soul of evangelical America.

Luke 4 is commonly referred to as Jesus's "inaugural address." Luke sets the scene: "When [Jesus] came to Nazareth, where he had been brought up, he went to the synagogue on the Sabbath day, as was his custom. He stood up to read, and the scroll of the prophet Isaiah was given to him." Next, Jesus reads from Isaiah 61: "He unrolled the scroll and found the place where it was written: 'The Spirit of the Lord is upon me, because he has anointed me to bring good news to the poor. He has sent me to proclaim release to the captives and recovery of sight to the blind, to let the oppressed go free, to proclaim the year of the Lord's favor.' " Then, Jesus places himself squarely in the meaning of the text: "And he rolled up the scroll, gave it back to the attendant, and sat down. The eyes of all in the synagogue were fixed on him. Then he began to say to them, 'Today this scripture has been fulfilled in your hearing.' "

A stark political reality stands behind this story. In the days of Jesus, the area we now call the Middle East was an occupied territory under the control of the Roman Empire. The Jews under this occupation had been waiting for the Messiah to come. In Isaiah and other prophetic books, when Jews lived under other oppressive empires, the prophets reported that God promised to send someone who would overturn the present order of the world and restore the order of God. That person would bring good news to the oppressed (Isaiah 61:1), he would rule with equity (Isaiah 11:4), and he would become the king over all kings (Isaiah 2:2–4 and Micah 4:1–5). The result of the Messiah's rule would be the restoration of shalom (Isaiah 52:7).

Jesus unrolled the Isaiah scroll and stopped at chapter 61. He read *that* passage. Why Isaiah 61? Why not Isaiah 6, which is about holiness? Why not Isaiah 44, which is about God's promise to bless Israel? Certainly Jesus's people needed encouragement in those days. However, Luke says Jesus chose *that* passage, and it is about good news to the poor, the marginalized, the imprisoned, and the oppressed. Nearly everyone except the ruling elites and their clients was oppressed. All outside the principalities and powers could point to Rome as their oppressor.

The ruling Judean oligarchy, headquartered in the Jerusalem Temple, collaborated with the Roman Empire. Its officials collected taxes for the empire and regularly charged exorbitant sums, keeping the extra to build their own fortunes. Herod had ruled in Judea for thirty-three years under a title given to him by the Roman senate: "King of the Jews." He expanded his territory by war and subjugation, building his tax base and collecting slaves as captives of war, a common practice of the time. He was among the best of Rome's client kings. He was known for his massive building projects, including his massive reconstruction of the Jerusalem Temple—in tribute to the pagan occupiers, he put the Roman eagle over the main entrance. The Sanhedrin governed Judea in civil and criminal matters. The high priest of the Sanhedrin was their elected leader. To oppose this Jerusalem oligarchy was also to oppose the authority of Rome, and Rome did not take insurrection lightly.[7]

When Jesus reads Isaiah 61, he is sending a political message to the powers of the empire. He announces a reversal of power both political and religious, embodied in his very own life, *today*. The God of Isaiah 61 lifts up the lowly and transforms them into the ones who rebuild the breached walls of desolated cities. Isaiah announces a Messiah who will champion the causes of the poor while tending to their daily, ordinary needs. He will bind up their broken hearts and heal them. He will release the captives. And he will proclaim "the year of the Lord's favor." Any Jew in the synagogue who heard Jesus read would have known that the year of favor was the time of Jubilee.[8]

Jubilee was a political and economic provision God instituted for the Israelites during the establishment of Israel (Leviticus 25). It was meant to ensure that no family in Israel would fall into generational cycles of poverty. Jubilee was a debt "reset" button to be pressed in Israel every fifty years, at the end of seven seven-year cycles. If a family fell into poverty and lost its home, its debt would be forgiven and the house would be restored to the original owner or the next of kin. If someone was taken into indentured servitude, the servant would be released and assets restored. The year of Jubilee was probably never actually carried out entirely, partly because of unintended consequences which hurt the poor—

for example, the paucity of loans available close to the year of forgiveness. However, everyone hearing Jesus at a time when poverty and destitution were increasing because of Roman taxation policies would have understood the political and economic implications of his claim, "Today this scripture has been fulfilled in your hearing."

Luke does not tell us if Jesus read the entire chapter, but his hearers would have known the entire text. They would have known the text makes two references to the Genesis creation stories. Isaiah 61:3 says, "They will be called oaks of righteousness, the planting of the Lord, to display his glory." "They" in the text refers to the poor, the brokenhearted, the oppressed, the captives, the prisoners. They "shall build up the ancient ruins" (Isaiah 61:4a). They "shall repair the ruined cities, the devastations of many generations" (Isaiah 61:4b). Isaiah proclaimed that the poor themselves would become the "oaks of righteousness," a metaphor for "justice" in Hebrew, planted and displayed for God's glory. There are two other trees in scripture that God plants: the tree of life and the tree of the knowledge of good and evil, both in Genesis 2. In referring to oaks of righteousness planted by God, Isaiah echoes the Genesis story of divinely created trees.

At the conclusion of Isaiah 61, the prophet makes a more explicit reference to Genesis 1–2. "For *as* the earth brings forth its shoots, and *as* a garden causes what is sown in it to spring up, *so* the Lord God will cause righteousness and praise to spring up before all the nations" (Isaiah 61:11). Isaiah rejoices because, in the same way that the earth brought forth its shoots (Genesis 1:12) and in the same way that a garden causes what is sown in it to spring up (Genesis 2:5), so too, God will cause justice and praise to spring *from* (Isaiah 61:3) the oppressed and all the nations will see it. When Jesus proclaimed that Isaiah 61 had been fulfilled as he read it, he tapped deep roots that drew their life from Genesis 1–2. To understand the significance of Jesus's inaugural address in Luke 4 requires unpacking the meaning behind Jesus's statement of his mission.

GENESIS 1–3

Whole libraries have been written to discern the Genesis texts, and interpretations of Genesis are important to Christianity, Judaism, and Islam. The evangelical perspective approaches the text with the assumption that it is possible to know the authors' intended meanings. My own interpretation, which follows, has roots in InterVarsity and incorporates church tradition and historical perspectives as resources for understanding the text more fully. It offers an evangelical understanding of Genesis 1–3 as a basis for understanding shalom as the roots of Luke 4.

Fundamentalists insist that the Genesis text is intended to be an historic scientific account of creation, a literally true account. I do not take Genesis 1 *literally*; I take it *literarily*. I approach the scripture as a literary document, and I seek out and trust the truth communicated through the text. Not all texts are the same; hence, to discern the meaning of a text requires discerning the kind of text it is. Is it story or explanation, parable or history, prose or poetry? Is it historic narrative or scientific theory? Like parables and stories, poetry is not meant to be interpreted *literally*. It does not attempt to communicate facts. Rather, it attempts to tell a deeper, richer, more complex truth. Poets use literary devices such as symbols, metaphor, simile, parallel structures, and repetition to communicate feeling and truth that transcend the literal meanings of words on the page or the bare bones of facts.

Genesis 1 is poetry, and should be read as poetry. This poetic reading does not detract from the truth of the text. Rather, it frees the reading from unintended entrapment in literal facts and allows deeper truths to rise to the surface. Reading poetry as a scientific theory or a historical record misses or trivializes the truth a writer was intending to communicate.[9]

Genesis 1:1–5 begins with an affirmation that God was there "in the beginning." God is not created but is the uncreated creator of all things. The "formless void" from which God creates can mean chaos or "to lay waste" in Hebrew. Verse two continues, "darkness covered the face of the deep, while a wind from God swept over the face of the water." Darkness carries poetic meanings of misery, destruction, death, ignorance, sorrow, or wickedness. The "deep" in Hebrew holds ancient understandings of primeval waters deep in the underworld or abyss, suggesting fear and mystery. The "wind" from God can also be translated "breath" or "spirit" of God and is grammatically feminine. The earth was a wasteland, full of misery, death, and destruction, and the breath of God hovered over a surging mass of chaos.[10]

From the chaos, God creates the world. God "speaks" and "and so it was." God begins by separating light from darkness. Then he separates the waters of the sea from the waters of the sky. Ancient Mesopotamian cosmologies pictured the sky as a solid dome of lapis lazuli that separated the waters above that fell on the earth from the waters below the earth that welled up. Reflecting that cosmology in Genesis,

God creates three domains: the dome of the heavens, the sky; next, the earth below; and, finally, the seas and the waters under the earth. Then, God fills each domain.

God not only speaks to bring things into being, but also declares that everything is "good," which in Hebrew can mean blessed, beautiful, delightful, and loving. At the end of the sixth day, everything made in creation is "very good." Once all living things are declared good, God also specifies that every living animal—wild animals, birds, reptiles, and humans—is to eat green plants, seeds, and fruit for food. From this vision of creation, the prophet Isaiah would later draw an image of peace in which lions and lambs could lie down together without fear. In the Hebrew understanding of the world found in Genesis, creation is not "very good" in the static sense that all tension, darkness, or blemish is absent. Rather, humanity is called to understand that all the relationships within creation are blessed, beautiful, delightful, and characterized by love, even in the presence of what terrifies human beings.

In creating the world, God does not do away with the darkness but limits it. God does not do away with the sea, which symbolized chaos; rather, God contains it, so that life can flourish. Then God makes the great sea monsters (Genesis 1:21), legendary and fearful creatures that symbolized the most frightening aspects of the cast oceans. By placing the sea monsters in the goodness of creation, the writer suggests that humans, created later, should appreciate even that which is frightening and threatening, even that which has the power to harm or kill. The sea monsters served humanity by being part of a world within which humans realized the limits of their own powers in relation to the vastness of creation and their need for God. Humans were drawn back to a relationship with God as they called on him for help, guidance, and protection in the mysterious, scary arenas of life on earth.

In Genesis 1:26–27 poetic form gives way to song: "God said, let *us* make humanity in *our* image and likeness [emphasis added] . . . So, God created humankind in his image, in the image of God he created them; male and female he created them." The traditional evangelical understanding of this passage focused its interpretation on the dominant relationship humans have over the rest of creation—humans were the high point of the creation story. However, the real punch of this text is that human beings are made in the image of God—both male and female together. As if to reiterate this point, God speaks as if he were plural, *us* and *our image and likeness*—not one over another, but two together.

In the ancient world of Mesopotamia, from which this Genesis text emerged, the gods, capricious and demanding, were to be feared and served. The power of the gods was seen in natural phenomena like the moon, the sun, the sea, or a mountain. These deities vied for power. They copulated, created, murdered, schemed, and treated humans as pawns in their heavenly conflicts or as slaves to do their labors. In this cultural context, the writer of Genesis breaks into song in verse 27 and offers another worldview that reverses how humans should see themselves and how they should see God. All humanity was made in the *image and likeness* of God. Hence, humans partners with God must act as God would act to exercise stewardship over creation. Women are co–image bearers of God and are the partners, not the property or domestic servants, of men. They share equal dominion over God's creation; their roles are not designated; they are defined in terms of co-dominion.

The word the author uses for "image," *tselem,* is noteworthy and means "representative figure." It usually referred to kings, who were seen as the representatives of God on earth. However, in Genesis 1:27, all men and women are God's representatives. By using the word *tselem*, the author of Genesis I claims that wherever humans stand, they represent divine authority and rule. Thus, as ones who bear the image of God, all humans are sacred creations. To bless another human being is to bless the image of God on earth. Likewise, to hit, to harm, or to oppress a human being is to hit, harm, or oppress the image of God on earth.

In Jesus's times, Caesar's *tselem* marked the territory where he reigned. His statue in the middle of the square, his image on a coin, his portrait on basilica walls, all would indicate that "Caesar reigns here." Every new emperor sent his image throughout the empire, and each community was supposed to greet the arriving image with a festival, called an *adventus,* as if the emperor himself were arriving. In effect, he was, since all oaths were sworn before the image. Hence, for Jesus to refer back to the creation story by reading Isaiah 61 would have been to deny Caesar his special rule.

God wove all of creation as a vast network of connected relationships, and humanity, made especially in the divine image, was called to love it, just as God loves it. Day and night provide time for humans to rest and work. The sun, moon, and stars help humans tell the seasons, making it possible to know when to reap and when to sow. In addition, humans were in right relationship with all the living beings of creation. Humanity's job was to multiply, fill the earth, and bless and help creation flourish.

God rested and took delight in his creation on the seventh day. Framing the creation story with the poetic structure of seven days, the writer suggests God's relationship with creation culminates in delight and rest. God's relationship with everything in the entire cosmos is extremely blessed, beautiful, delightful, and characterized by emphatic love of all that exists. Thus, love, servanthood, faithfulness, reciprocity, and care characterize the ties that bind each part of creation to the other and God to all creation.

When Jesus stands in the synagogue and quotes Isaiah 61, which contains the allusion to Genesis 1—"For as the earth brings forth its shoots, and as a garden causes what is sown in it to spring up, so the Lord God will cause righteousness and praise to spring up before all the nations" (Isaiah 61:11)—he reminds his hearers of how God took chaos and created order. God took a wasteland and brought forth beauty and life. God had done this before, he could do it again. Jesus declares to the powers that their exploitation of God's creation is about to end, as God takes back what is his for those made in his image. As Jesus reads the text, he proclaims that the restoration of relationships between creator and all created beings and powers has begun.

Genesis 2 is written as a story. It has a different point from Genesis 1. Genesis 2 offers a more detailed, intimate account of how humans came to be. In this account, God touched and molded humanity from the clay of the earth, like a sculptor. The earth, *ha-adamah,* is shaped into *ha-adam,* literally, a being made of earth. God breathed life into the human being's nostrils and put the creature into a vast, abundant garden, *gan-eden,* which means garden of delight. The English version translates the Hebrew into the proper name Eden. The garden overflowed with life.

In verse 9, God planted two trees in the middle of

the garden: "Out of the ground the Lord God made to grow every tree that is pleasant to the sight and good for food, the tree of life also in the midst of the garden, and the tree of the knowledge of good and evil." Unlike Genesis 1, where the earth brings forth vegetation, in Genesis 2 God plants the two trees. God is a gardener. In verse 16, God gives the human a warning: "You may freely eat of every tree of the garden; but of the tree of knowledge of good and evil you shall not eat, for in the day that you eat of it you shall die."

The text begs the question of why God would put a fruit tree in the middle of the garden of delight that would kill those who ate of it. Here lies a core distinction between Genesis 1 and Genesis 2. While Genesis 1 flows as a sweeping epic outlining all the relationships created by God, Genesis 2 brings human relationships with God and with each other to the foreground, though it also describes the relationship of humans to the rest of creation. As such, a prominent evangelical view of Genesis 2 is that the tree of the knowledge of good and evil was necessary for paradise to be complete. If the Hebrew view of creation is that all relationships are characterized by love, then there is no greater love relationship than the relationship between God and humanity. God is creator, while humans are creatures. Hence, God is other: mysterious and sometimes a source of awe-inspired fear.

There is a plethora of views concerning the significance of the tree of the knowledge of good and evil. Some contend the fruit itself was evil. Others propose the fruit represents something in modern life. Personally, I do not believe the tree itself is evil, nor do I believe its fruit represents any object or action in the modern world. It is simply a tree, but this particular tree has a warning attached—words from God. The tree grants the knowledge of good and evil not through its fruit but through the choice that it offers the man and woman. I contend that if humanity was created to love God, who already loved humanity, then for humanity's love to be real, God had to give human beings a way to choose or to spurn that relationship. To discard the lover's commandment would reveal a deficit of trust and of love. To choose the tree is to reject the one who loves them. The tree serves as the one place that draws humans back into a love relationship with God, the other.

Chapter 3 of Genesis is the hinge point of the human story. In chapter 2 God had created both man and woman. They love and take delight in each other, and they are naked and unafraid. Genesis 3 begins:

> Now the serpent was more crafty than any other wild animal that the Lord God had made. He said to the woman, "Did God say, 'You shall not eat from any tree in the garden?' " The woman said to the serpent, "We may eat of the fruit of the trees in the garden; but God said, 'You shall not eat of the fruit of the tree that is in the middle of the garden, nor shall you touch it, or you shall die.' " But the serpent said to the woman, "You will not die for God knows that when you eat of it your eyes will be opened, and you will be like God, knowing good and evil." (Genesis 3:1–5)

The serpent offered the man and woman a chance to be like God through the power of knowledge. This is a counteroffer to God's love.

> So, when the woman saw that the tree was good for food, and that it was a delight to the eyes, and that

the tree was to be desired to make one wise, she took of its fruit and ate; and she also gave some to her husband, who was with her, and he ate. Then the eyes of both were opened, and they knew that they were naked: and they sewed fig leaves together and made loincloths for themselves. (Genesis 3:6–7)

The serpent was in rebellion against God. In pre-Fall paradise, the serpent was there. For centuries scholars have wrestled over what the serpent actually was. The text gives no definitive description. This created being approached other created beings and swayed them to follow its way. Its way was the way of knowledge without love. The serpent used the tree to lure humanity away from love for God and into a power struggle with God.

The humans had a choice. They could have chosen to love. Instead, they chose not to trust their lover God and reached for the power offered by one more like themselves, a creature also. They accepted the serpent's lie and chose to pursue a futile attempt to be like God in his knowledge of good and evil. The tragic irony is that the man and the woman were already made *in God's image.* That image is what set them apart from the rest of creation in Genesis 1. It was the hallmark of their humanity, but they only bore the *image* of God. They were not the same as God.

Miroslav Volf says those made in the image of God are to be "in some significant sense like God . . . 'in true righteousness and holiness' (Ephesians 4:24), like God in loving enemies (Matthew 5:44)."[11] God is the ultimate lover. By nature, he has no need to strive for power; rather, he leverages his power to love his enemies. The man and the woman, made in the image of God, had the ability to love the other. Yet, when they grasped only at knowledge as power, their ability to love faltered. Therefore, what distinguishes God from humanity is God's ability to encounter evil and retain his ability to love the other. Somehow when humans experience evil they distort the image of God in their souls and create deep deficits in their capacity to love—especially to love that which is other. 1 John 4:16 makes the reality of God plain: "God is love and those who abide in love abide in God."

The man and the woman grasped at godlikeness, and as a result, the very thing they reached for, which they already possessed, the image of God within them, was lost. Yet their choice did not affect only them; they lived within the community of creation. Twice, soldiers have confessed to me that, after experiencing the evils of war, the job of their lives was to "become human again." They had lost the ability to love—to love themselves, to love others, to love God, to love the rest of creation, and even to love life itself. Shalom says all parts are linked to the whole. No created being lives in isolation from the others. So, when one relationship falters, all relationships suffer.

When the man and the woman broke their relationship with God, every other relationship that was declared very good came tumbling down. One after another, the loving relationships God established were corrupted. The first relationship to break was human relationships within themselves. According to Genesis 3:7 shame and self-hatred entered the world. The second relationship to tumble was the human relationship with God (Genesis 3:8–12). For the first time, humans hid from God, and the man blamed everyone else for his choice when he said, "That woman you gave to be with me." Next, the relationship between men and women collapsed (Genesis 3:16–19). The consequence of seeking the power of knowledge without love is that the man and the woman, naked and unashamed, lost the trust, intimacy, and safety they once shared. Subsequently, the relationship between humanity and the rest of creation was twisted (Genesis 3:15). For the first time, an animal physically struck out at a human being. Also for the first time, working the earth included pain, toil, and futility (Genesis 3:17–19). This cascade of disasters corrupted the relationship between systems and human beings. In both Genesis 1 and 2, all relationships in a created order worked together for the good of all. These systems were corrupted at the Fall, and human relationships with systems became filled with strife and pain. Finally, death entered the world (Genesis 3:21) and God killed the first animal to cover humanity's shame. Then God drove the humans out of paradise, lest they eat from the tree of life and live forever under such corrupt conditions. The rest of the Bible documents the negative effects of corrupted relationships: brothers slay each other, nations war, and ethnic divisions cause deep enmity.

Biblical scholar Walter Brueggemann warns that we must not lose sight of the fact that God is the creator and bedrock of shalom.[12] Shalom is dependent on God for its realization, not human will. Any society which attempts to realize shalom without God will fail, because it will severely underestimate the forces of oppression, destruction, and chaos in our world. When humans confront evil on the level of war, colonialism, imperialism, ethnic cleansing, gender domination, deadly epidemics, and environmental degradation and disasters, they will inevitably find they fail to stop them—manage them maybe, but not stop them.

I took a pilgrimage to Germany, Croatia, Bosnia, and Serbia in the summer of 2004 with a community of students and InterVarsity staff. We went to understand the substance of peacemaking and the substance of peace breaking. One thing became clear: as we walked the gravel-strewn grounds of the first Nazi concentration camp in Dachau, Germany, and saw the words "Never Again" etched in stone in five different languages, we had hope. Next, we rode sunflower-lined highways on the road to Vukovar, Croatia. Our guide explained, "The sunflowers are so tall because the fields haven't been plowed for a decade. Mines are still out there hidden by the flowers." We continued through the mountainside of Bosnia to pay homage to the dead at Srebrenica. Eight thousand men and boys died there, all in one day, during the Bosnian war. At the entrance to the cemetery was a large stone monument. It included the declaration "Never Again." We were told that war was happening again in Sudan, and the Darfur genocide was just beginning to take hold. It was clear to us: humanity left to its own devices will misuse power and make itself an idol. When that happens, the image of God is crushed on earth and the ability to love the other is crippled.

Some would counter that both sides in these wars claim a divine mandate and that the presence of religion is part of the problem. They would say that Christianity causes wars because it is a monopolistic monotheism that claims it has the truth exclusively. It is true that religion has been used as a potent divisive and violent force. However, secular ideologies have fueled their own wars and oppressive systems. Wars, whatever their ideological rationales, are caused by a desire to dominate others in order to secure or horde resources. In Bosnia, Slobodan Milosevic sought to claim Bosnia's land and resources for Serbia. In Darfur, herdsmen and farmers disputed over water rights. The Jewish Holocaust itself was not about religion. It was triggered by Germany's economic hardships following World War I and the country's decision to scapegoat Jews, socialist Christians, homosexuals, and the disabled by identifying them as the reason for the country's economic decline. These societies attempted to dominate others in an attempt to secure their own power and resources.

For Christians, the humans' relationship with God was based in love, not force or a legal contract. Consequently, God did not bind them to his side. Their choice was allowed to stand, and shalom ceased. However, this is not the end of the story. There is good news. The rest of scripture chronicles God's pursuit of reconciliation with his beloved creation and the restoration of every relationship broken at the Fall.

That pursuit is writ large in the life of Jesus Christ. To appreciate the implications of Jesus's inaugural address, we must plumb the deep resonances of Isaiah 61 with the Genesis creation accounts. Genesis 1 promises that, just as creation sprang up from the earth, so too, justice and praise will spring forth from the oppressed. In Genesis 2 the reader is introduced to God, the gardener, who is intimately connected with his creation. He kisses humanity to life and then plants two trees in the garden: the tree of life and the tree of the knowledge of good and evil. Brueggemann insisted that only God can enact shalom. According to Isaiah, God will do it; according to Jesus, it is being done. Humanity's original use of the tree to choose power over love in an attempt to find peace is set in ironic juxtaposition to the truth of how God's glory is established. It is established as God enacts the power of his love.

THE POWER OF JESUS'S CROSS AND RESURRECTION: EPHESIANS 1 AND 2

The letter to the Ephesians uses two images to unveil the power of the cross and resurrection, death and the wall of hostility between people groups:

> You were *dead* through the trespasses and sins in which you once lived, *following the course of this world*, following the ruler of the power of the air, the spirit that is now at work among those who are disobedient. All of us once lived among them in the passions of our flesh, following the desires of the flesh and senses, and we were by nature children of wrath, like everyone else. (Ephesians 2:1–3, italics added)

Ever since the Fall, the world has tried to find its own peace that has led to death. *"But* now in Christ Jesus you who were once far off have been brought near by the blood of Christ. For he is our *peace*; in his flesh he has made both groups into one and has broken down *the dividing wall*, that is the *hostility* between us" (Ephesians 2:13–14, italics added).

The Greek word for peace is *eirene*, and it is used for the Hebrew *shalom*. So, Jesus himself is *eirene* or *shalom*. Ephesians uses the ethnic hatred between the Jews and the gentiles as an object lesson to show Jesus's power to bring shalom. "The dividing wall that is the hostility between us" refers to a specific wall. The Temple was separated into multiple courts. A court for the gentiles lay around the outer perimeter. The court for Jewish women was inside the gentile area and inside that was the court for the Jewish men.

Tradition says the innermost court, called the "holy of holies," was where God lived and where only ordained priests could go. The wall that separated the gentile court from the Jewish courts read "Enter on pain of death."

Ephesians says Jesus is our *eirene*. Jesus is the solution for the wall of hostility and for death.

> I pray that the God of our Lord Jesus Christ, the Father of glory, *may give you a spirit of wisdom and revelation* as you come to know him, so that with the eyes of your heart enlightened, you may know what is the hope to which he has called you, what are the riches of his glorious inheritance among the saints, and what is the immeasurable greatness of his power for us who believe, according to the working of his great power. God put this power for us who believe, according to the working of his great power. God put this power to work in Christ when he *raised him from the dead* and seated him at his right hand in the heavenly places far above all rule and authority and power and dominion and above every name that is named, not only in this age but also in the age to come. And *he has put all things under his feet* and has made him the head over all things for the church, which is his body, the fullness of him who fills all in all. (Ephesians 1:17–23, italics added)

The text tells Christians in a church in an important city experiencing ethnic strife that the power of their faith is not being put to good use. That power to heal broken relationships is demonstrated in Jesus's resurrection. In other words, the significance of the resurrection is not just how it justifies individuals before God. When Jesus beat death, he reversed the power of the Fall. He beat the strongest power in our world—death—the one power all humanity must face at one point. The text tells us death is now "under his feet." And because of the resurrection, *all things* are under Jesus's feet. This means the hostility between ethnic groups and nations is under Jesus's feet, and the hostility within families is under Jesus's feet. The hostility between humans and the rest of creation is under Jesus's feet. The hostility between humans and their systems and between men and women is under Jesus's feet. The hostility within our very selves is under Jesus's feet. And finally, the hostility between humanity and God is under Jesus's feet. To say that these hostilities are under his feet means that Jesus's death on the cross and his resurrection make it possible for all the relationships broken at the Fall to be restored. Because God is the force behind shalom and the Gospels say Jesus is God, Ephesians declares that following Jesus makes the restoration of shalom possible: "For he himself is our shalom."

This shalom is the good news evangelical leaders are beginning to embrace. It is a conception of the good news that engages the powers and structures that seek to crush the image of God on earth. It requires work at every level and it requires faith because shalom is ultimately not the work of human hands. It is the work of God. It is the work of Jesus, who is God and human joined in one flesh. Humans are called to partner with God in stewarding his creation and in restoring this fallen world. Evangelicals are beginning to believe again that partnering with God means we must work to restore the reign of God over *all* things, which brings with it the restoration of shalom to *all* things.

8

Engage

Ain't gonna let nobody
turn me 'roun, turn me 'roun, turn me 'roun
Ain't gonna let nobody
turn me 'roun
I'm gonna keep on a-walkin'
keep on a-talkin'
walkin' into freedom land.

—civil rights song based on
traditional African American spiritual

Jeff Farmer, president of the Open Bible Churches—a seventy-five-year-old Pentecostal and charismatic denomination based in Iowa—said in a recent interview,

> Pentecostals and evangelicals have always recognized sin as being personal, but much of the leadership, and certainly the people sitting in the pews, have not understood that sin can also be social. So, when we think about salvation and redemption in Christ, we always think of it as a personal thing, rather than social redemption that would address in-

stitutional structural sin. Of course, the prophets addressed it. Jesus addressed it. Yet, in our zeal for con-
verting people and fulfilling the Great Commission
[Matthew 28:19–20], we have missed the reality that
sin can be both personal and social. Only now are we
beginning to recognize there is a need for us to engage at a totally different level.[1]

Farmer explained that the evangelical church is encounter-
ing a hinge point in history where a new understanding of the
good news, pointing to Luke 4 and Isaiah 61, is altering the
way it engages with public life and politics.

In my interviews with evangelical leaders I was struck by
the impact of this shift on the positions they are taking on
major national issues. For example, when asked how their understanding of the good news impacts their position on gay
marriage or civil union legislation, the vast majority of respondents said they would support legislation that all people
are made in the image of God and thus are endowed with inalienable human rights. Thus, they would support gay people's right to civil unions. However, in most cases, they viewed
marriage as a religious sacrament and would advocate the
right of religious institutions to define the institution of marriage. Likewise, most respondents said their position on the
Iraq war was informed by Jesus's call in Matthew 5 to "Love
your enemies." Most could see no way the Iraq war met that
criterion or the moral standards of a just war. They oppose the
war. When asked how their understanding of the good news
affects their understanding of public assistance to the poor,
the majority of respondents referenced Matthew 25, Luke 4,
or Isaiah 61 directly, saying scripture commands that the
church work toward the abolition of poverty. Many referred

to the year of Jubilee as evidence that both the church and government must take responsibility for the poor.

HOPE

On June 28, 2006, everyone knew U.S. Senator Barack Obama (D-IL) was scheduled to speak that morning, but no one knew what he was going to say—not even Jim Wallis, who had invited him to the Sojourners/Call to Renewal Pentecost 2006 Conference.[2] Conference participants had heard from Hillary Clinton, Sam Brownback, Howard Dean, and others. Obama was scheduled to speak on the final morning as he accepted the Sojourners Joseph Award for faithful service in government.

Obama was the fifth black senator ever to serve in the United States Senate. His keynote speech at the 2004 Democratic National Convention catapulted him to center stage in politics. These words in particular served to give him visibility:

> E pluribus unum: "Out of many, one". . . . The pundits like to slice and dice our country into red states and blue states; red states for Republicans, blue states for Democrats. But I've got news for them, too. We worship an awesome God in the blue states and we don't like federal agents pokin' around in our libraries in the red states. . . . We are one people, all of us pledging allegiance to the Stars and Stripes, all of us defending the United States of America.[3]

Two years later, when Obama entered the sanctuary of the National City Christian Church in Washington, DC, the air was electric. He had yet to declare his candidacy in the 2008 presidential election, but as Wallis introduced him and Obama made the long walk from the front pew to the podium, I remember thinking we may be in the presence of a future president of the United States. With each stride he seemed to be walking in a realm of his own, as if he was a figure come to speak from the future to the present.

Obama began by congratulating Sojourners/Call to Renewal on their excellent job crafting "A Covenant for a New America." The "Covenant" is an ecumenical initiative, spearheaded by Sojourners and triggered by the devastation of Hurricane Katrina and the poverty and neglect it revealed. In a 2006 interview, Jeff Carr, then chief operations officer of Sojourners, explained the genesis of the "Covenant." He and Wallis spent Labor Day weekend of 2005 on the phone, as they watched the pictures flash across CNN and MSNBC.[4] CNN anchor Anderson Cooper dropped his newsperson veneer during a live interview with Sen. Mary Landrieu (D-LA). The senator boasted of a bill Congress was about to pass that would keep FEMA and the Red Cross up and running; Cooper interrupted her and said that it was not a time to be self-congratulatory. Dead bodies were floating in the streets. Cooper referred to a female body floating over forty-eight hours that was being eaten by rats. "I mean, there are people who want answers," Cooper demanded, "and there are people who want someone to stand up and say, 'You know what? We should have done more. Are all the assets being brought to bear?' "[5]

Carr and Wallis realized that this confrontation was different from anything they had seen before. America was seeing, up close, in their living rooms, the devastation and hopelessness of poverty exacerbated by the underresourced state of the poor . . . in the richest nation in the world. So-journers shifted the theme of its annual gathering of religious leaders that Thanksgiving and crafted "The Katrina Pledge," which called on leaders to pledge to be personally involved and to work for sweeping change of the nation's priorities. Next came the "Covenant," which provided a road map to overcoming poverty through religious commitment and political leadership. With more than thirty organizations endorsing it, the pledge created a platform for Sojourners' antipoverty work on Capitol Hill.[6]

Obama continued his address at the Pentecost 2006 Conference, calling religious America and secular America to address the mutual suspicion between them. For, Obama noted, that was the crux of the problem. Mutual suspicion has kept shalom-minded people from engaging in public life.[7]

MUTUAL SUSPICION

Within evangelical America, three factors contribute to a tenuous connection between religion and politics: a too-close collusion with the Republican Party, attacks on undecided evangelicals, and Democratic avoidance of religion. The Religious Right's alliance with the Republican Party in the 1980s framed it as "the Christian party." Thus, the tide of Republican sentiment within evangelical America was so fierce that undecided evangelicals risked having their faith called into question if they raised questions about the two hottest buttons the Religious Right pressed incessantly—abortion and homosexuality. Without political leadership beyond the Religious Right, undecided evangelicals tended to vote with the tide or they did not vote at all. The Democratic

Party's response to the Religious Right played into conservative hands. Democrats excised all mention of religion and
faith from political discourse and demonized those who discussed faith in public. This further alienated undecided
evangelicals, leading them to believe the hype of the Religious Right.

Unaligned evangelicals lacked two things: a political alternative to the Republican Party and the leadership without
party allegiance to guide them on how to apply faith to issues.
In the absence of such authentic faithful leadership, these
unaligned evangelicals either followed the crowd every four
years during presidential election seasons or they checked
out of the political process altogether.

These two responses left issues of religion and politics to
two major constituencies: Religious Right ideologues and
those committed to a secular state, who sought to counter
the Religious Right hegemony. Politics tended to be polarized into Religious Right and secular, but few practical solu-
tions were offered for undecided evangelicals. Though many
people committed to a secular public sphere want to keep
faith out of public discourse and policy, this pushes the
power of religious motivations for many people's choices un-
derground. Open debate and discussion on religion earlier
characterized U.S. history. Diverse public discussion of religion and politics requires religious people to defend their political positions in relation to reason and concrete evidence,
such as constitutional law or science. It also requires them to
make their positions intelligible to other religions and to
nonreligious people, since appeals to supernatural authority
carry no weight in an open democracy. America is a pluralis-
tic society, and as such, religious people need to engage the
public square in a way that communicates respect for the

other and seeks the common good, grounded in their religious values.

Obama noted what historians of religion in America know: almost every major reform movement in U.S. history was ignited by people passionate and vocal about their faith. He called on progressives to shed their biases and recognize the presence of overlapping values that are shared by both religious and secular people. He then demonstrated what is required of people of faith in a democracy:

> We might recognize that the call to sacrifice on behalf of the next generation, the need to think in terms of "thou" and not just "I," resonates with religious congregations all across the country. And we might realize that we have the ability to reach out to the evangelical community and engage millions of religious Americans in the larger project of American renewal.[8]

Obama saw what many other Democrats had failed to see, that the Religious Right does not speak for all people of faith in America and certainly not all Christians. In fact, the Right only makes up a small segment of evangelicals in the United States. What is needed is leadership for the rest. Obama filled that need when he spoke as a faithful citizen who holds public office in a democracy:

> Democracy demands that the religiously motivated translate their concerns into universal, rather than religion-specific, values. It requires that their proposals be subject to argument, and amenable to reason. I may be opposed to abortion for religious

reasons, but if I seek to pass a law banning the practice, I cannot simply point to the teachings of my church or evoke God's will. I have to explain why abortion violates some principle that is accessible to people of all faiths, including those with no faith at all.[9]

Obama told the story of Abraham and Isaac to make his point. Abraham heard from God that he was to sacrifice his son, Isaac. Abraham, with uncompromising faith, had to act. "But it's fair to say that if any of us leaving this church saw Abraham on a roof of a building raising his knife, we would, at the very least, call the police and expect the Department of Children and Family Services to take Isaac away from Abraham." Obama said those who did not share Abraham's faith would not hear what Abraham heard, or see what Abraham saw: "The best we can do is act in accordance with those things that we all see, and that we all hear, be it common laws or basic reason."[10] Obama called on both the faithful and secular communities to engage the public square with "fair-minded words." He admitted that his own Web site had used Democratic "boilerplate language" to explain his position on abortion. Thus he, too, was guilty of polarizing politics. Obama repented. He replaced the statement with fair-minded words, still in support of a woman's right to choose, but not antagonistic toward pro-life positions. He was reminded there is a large segment of citizens who want "a deeper, fuller conversation about religion in this country."[11]

Obama received a standing ovation. He had opened a way for religious people and nonreligious people to work together for social change. I turned to the woman sitting next to me, Kenya De Alamapo, an African American twenty-something from Philadelphia, and said, "We have just witnessed history."

ACTIVATED FAITHFULS

De Alamapo lives in a racially and economically diverse community, the brainchild of Philadelphia's former mayor, John F. Street, a devout Christian. Street, who was mayor from 2000 until 2008, implemented a plan to rebuild Philadelphia. It called for the renovation of approximately 85,000 abandoned homes, turning them into mixed-income development units. This plan allowed De Alamapo, who grew up in poverty, to own her first home. She told me that the day of the opening felt like a church service as Street gave credit for the idea to God, saying God simply used him as a vessel.[12]

De Alamapo shared her vision with the Sojourners conference attendees, a vision of *koinonia* (fellowship): "The Lord has given me this vision of living in community with people that come from diverse ethnic, racial, and economic backgrounds. That was one of the things that drew me to the Christian faith."[13] De Alamapo explained that the foundation of her faith comes from the example of those first faithful believers, whose story is told in the book of Acts. Those early Christians practiced the Three Rs, reconciliation across ethnic barriers, relocation into diverse community, and redistribution, as everyone sold what they had and distributed their resources to all who had need. "My understanding of the Gospels," said De Alamapo, "is not just the good news of personal salvation but the good news that the kingdom of God has come. With the kingdom, a new relationship is lifted among the members."[14]

Sitting behind De Alamapo was Kevin Saunders, a law

student at Boston University. While teaching high school in Jonesborough, Arkansas, he was struck by the educational disparity between the affluent and the impoverished. Saunders went to law school to learn more about how to address the issues of systemic injustice and is now working with Partners in Health, a secular organization that works toward community-based health care in developing countries. Saunders said, "To me, it's personal. It's my faith. It's important because politics are a statement about who we are and how we want the world to be."[15]

Jesse Lava is co-founder and executive director of FaithfulDemocrats.com, a national Web site based in Chicago. He was sitting toward the rear as Obama gave his speech. Lava, who grew up with a secular Jewish father and lapsed Catholic mother, chose an Episcopal church in which to begin his search for God. He found Jesus at a Christmas Eve service shortly after his mother passed away from colon cancer when he was seventeen. He investigated the teachings of Jesus for a year before deciding to be baptized. Around the same time, Lava went to Wesleyan University, where he got involved in politics. Lava said, "My faith affects my politics. I want to spread the light of God, the Holy Spirit throughout the world." Spread it he has.[16]

David Wilhelm, former Democratic National Committee (DNC) chair, teamed up with Lava. Wilhelm, a Christian, once delivered a speech to the Christian Coalition in his role as chair of the DNC. He told the coalition that a good Christian could belong to any political party. He was greeted with jeers. In the wake of the 2004 elections, Wilhelm and Lava noticed there were lots of Republican forums created to help Christians engage their platform issues and there were great groups doing nonpartisan progressive work, Sojourners and the Interfaith Alliance among them. However, they could not find any arena set aside specifically for Christians who were Democrats to wrestle with the issues that accepted faith as part of the equation. So, they created the online blogging community FaithfulDemocrats.com (FD). The moniker means Faithful to Jesus and Democrat. Lava and Wilhelm do not believe Christians should be Democrats. They simply recognized the need for leadership, which Obama outlined in his speech.[17]

Though Obama's 2006 speech was not the inspiration for FaithfulDemocrats.com, when Lava looks back on the Obama speech in 2007, he considered it a turning point. He explains: "Here we were, a year and a half after the Democrats had failed miserably to convey a sense of faith and values of the American people, and one of the leading Democrats in the country, Barack Obama, was very articulately and very powerfully conveying a sense of faith and values to the American people."[18] Lava believes the Obama speech had a direct effect on the launch of FaithfulDemocrats.com. The speech "gave legitimacy" to the idea of such a Web presence. "I think a lot of people were skeptical of even the existence of a Religious Left." As Lava noted, often secular political activists think when liberals talk about faith, they are being disingenuous: "It's almost inconceivable to them that we liberals could be doing it for anything other than for political reasons. . . . I think the obvious sincerity and the obvious power of Barack's speech upped the credibility of what we were doing."[19]

FaithfulDemocrats.com launched in September 2006 with an array of top Christian writers, journalists, theologians, historians, and activists logging in to share their thoughts each day. FD immediately gained credibility as a useful forum for discussion. I was among that original group of writers who sat nervously waiting for faceless people across the country to engage with our issues. In its first month alone, our blogging seemed to grant permission to a large segment of evangelical America to wrestle with the validity and viability of conservative Republican Party orthodoxies concerning abortion, gay marriage, stem-cell research, and the war in Iraq. It was clear something was shifting in evangelical America, and we were witnessing it firsthand. People openly questioned standard party lines, most for the first time. They were looking for guidance or simply a place to wrestle with ideas. The blog also became a storehouse of ideas for reporters and television stations that did not know where to get such information elsewhere. There were even some articles, Lava explains, "where reporters almost lifted language from our Web site word for word, which is great, because we want to provide that kind of resource." Lava sees FD as "one little square in the broad quilt of activism that made the Democrats' victory in 2006 possible."[20]

Sojourners' God's Politics.com joined the blogosphere days after FD. It expanded the dialogue with headliners like Jim Wallis, Brian McClaren, Tony Campolo, Diane Butler-Bass, Amy Sullivan, and other "Red-Letter Christians," even Ralph Reed of the Christian Coalition. God's Politics.com captured the attention of Christian and secular America. With the dual success of FaithfulDemocrats.com and God's Politics.com, it became clear: the blogosphere is prime territory for activism and advocacy among evangelical Americans.

Other evangelicals have focused their work for change on a particular issue. David P. Gushee believes Christians should care about human rights: "God is the author of life and human beings are made in God's image."[21] He notes that Christians are commanded to love their neighbors—even enemy neighbors; that Jesus died for all humanity; and that Christians should exercise responsibility as citizens through their influence as Christians. Gushee, chair of Evangelicals for Human Rights and distinguished professor of Christian ethics at McAfee School of Theology, wrote a February 2006 cover story for *Christianity Today* titled "Five Reasons Torture Is Always Wrong: And Why There Should Be No Exceptions." It was one of few evangelical articles on the subject published in early 2006, when the issue of torture moved to the forefront of American consciousness. Consequently, the National Religious Campaign Against Torture asked Gushee to write a statement against torture that could galvanize evangelicals, the base of the Bush administration's support, to stand and be counted on this issue.

Gushee led a group that took approximately one year to craft the statement. In the process, Evangelicals for Human Rights was developed as a nonprofit agency through which the statement about torture and messaging on other human rights issues could be disseminated to the public. To date, more than three hundred evangelical leaders have signed the statement, though he concedes these signatures are mostly from what he calls "the evangelical left and center."[22] The Right has resisted. Gushee notes, "I think that their inability to break with the Bush administration on torture exposes a loyalty to the Republican Party that is unhealthy. Our loyalty should be to Christ and to the teachings of the Bible. If you can't say no when it's time to say no, then you expose that your loyalties are confused."[23]

Gushee believes the human rights issue has great potential to be a bipartisan one and, in some cases, already is:

"Evangelicals have been enormously effective over the past decade as they've motivated Washington politicians to engage issues like the AIDS crisis in Africa, religious freedom issues around the world, global compassion concerns, debt relief, and current-day slavery."[24] This is evidence that evangelicals know better than to tolerate torture. He works toward the day when loyalty to Jesus will step to the forefront and trump loyalty to party politics.

Rachel Anderson, executive director of the Boston Faith & Justice Network and former student leader in InterVarsity, was also in the room when Obama spoke. She, too, was inspired. Only a year and a half earlier, she had approached Jim Wallis after a lecture at Harvard University, where Anderson earned her law and theology degrees. She wanted to find out if he knew of any justice-oriented groups, like Sojourners, in Boston. He knew of none, but he passed Anderson's name on to Christa Mazonne, the Sojourners' national field organizer. Mazonne had received several calls from Bostonians asking the same question. She decided to contact them all and suggest they get together. They did.

Over the course of the next year, the group of four multiplied as they focused on a key need in Boston. There were lots of ecumenical networks for justice in Boston, but evangelicals were largely uninvolved. All of the people Sojourners connected were evangelicals. They began with house meetings that always included prayer. Next, they launched worship focused on issues of justice and had small-group breakout sessions. Soon, small groups on economic stewardship sprang up. Over the last two and a half years, the Boston Faith & Justice Network has ignited an evangelical justice movement in Boston. "When we started," Anderson remembers, "the thing I heard again and again was, 'I thought I was the only one being drawn to justice. Now I'm part of a community that's actively engaging the issues!' "[25] Anderson was recently at a Christian conference where a young woman shared, "As a young person it's not assumed that I'll be a person of faith. So, if I am a believer, my faith has to be authentic. For me, that means serving the poor."[26]

At the time of the Obama speech, Jennifer Kottler was deputy director of Protestants for the Common Good, a Chicago-based advocacy group. Kottler grew up with "traditional white Midwest understanding of the good news," as she put it in a recent interview.[27] Yet, there was always something in her that knew there's more to faith than just personal transformation. When an African American co-worker invited Kottler to attend church with her one Sunday in Alexandria, Virginia, Kottler said yes. "Immediately, I said to myself, 'This is where I belong! This is how I understand the gospel.' "[28] Kottler is currently executive director of the Let Justice Roll Living Wage Campaign. It is a nonpartisan coalition of more than ninety organizations, including faith communities, community boards, labor groups, and business organizations committed to raising the minimum wage. Their bottom line is "A job should keep you out of poverty, not keep you in it."[29]

These are just a few of the faith-based advocacy movements igniting evangelicals at the grassroots level. These grassroots movements join international advocates like World Vision, International Justice Mission (IJM), and Bread for the World in their commitment to addressing issues of injustice on a policy level. World Vision, the compassionate NGO famous for its pictures of starving Ethiopian children in the 1980s, moved into the realm of human rights advocacy throughout the 1990s. IJM and Bread for the World both rose to prominence at the turn of the twenty-first century. They are key advocacy agencies helping connect Christians to issues of human rights and hunger, respectively. There are many more. What makes these movements different from other twentieth-century evangelical community-development efforts is that their work for shalom moves beyond the private realms of traditional mission. These new, politically engaged evangelicals are working in public life and politics, much like our forebearers of the nineteenth century. Their vision of shalom and evangelical faith are compelling them to engage the powers that create policies. They understand that public policies have potential to bless or curse, to give or steal from the others among them—others made in the image of God. Their movements are growing and having an impact.

The Obama speech was indeed an historic moment for evangelicals. Obama opened the door and a grassroots movement of shalom-minded evangelicals walked through to the other side.

RICHARD CIZIK AND THE NATIONAL ASSOCIATION OF EVANGELICALS

Most Americans who are familiar with the National Association of Evangelicals (NAE) probably remember the disgraceful exit its former leader, Ted Haggard, in the fall of 2006. Haggard's personal scandal with a male prostitute cast shadows of corruption and hypocrisy over the face of the entire organization. Nevertheless, the NAE has been a major force behind the shift in evangelical worldview through Richard Cizik's work on creation care and global warming.

At the March 2007 NAE meeting in Minneapolis,

months after Haggard's exit, a tectonic shift rumbled under the feet of delegates. The NAE board rejected a petition from Focus on the Family leader James Dobson and two dozen other high-profile conservative evangelicals to fire Cizik, NAE vice president of governmental affairs. Instead, the board affirmed its position that environmental steward-ship matters. The move signaled a definitive shift in the evan-gelical base of power.

Cizik explained in a 2007 interview, "My critics are say-ing, 'You're trying to alter the definition of "evangelical" away from political and economic conservatism.' Well, I'm sorry, but that's not the definition of 'evangelical' to begin with!"[30] He explained that evangelicals have to acknowledge that "we are in some respects, as N.T. Wright says, Neoplatonists, al-most modern-day Gnostics, who have, in our mistakenness of the gospel, become dualists." Cizik explains that some in the early church "subordinated its proper understanding of cre-ation to a Neoplatonic view that made the spirit important and the earth not important. . . . As such, Neoplatonism has contributed to bad stewardship, stupid economics, and a be-trayal of our true biblical responsibilities to the creation."[31] Cizik, who considers himself a conservative, says this world-view has led to environmentally destructive actions tanta-mount to taking what God has given humanity and flinging it back in his face.[32]

When asked why his stance on creation care led Dobson and other leaders to try to have him fired, Cizik explained, "The creation care issue is a frontal assault on the old world-view. And the old guard understands it as such."[33] Cizik, who promotes evangelical concerns on Capitol Hill, says a trans-formation of evangelicals' perception of the good news is definitely taking place. He mentioned a two-part study the

NAE conducted in partnership with sociologist John Green, of Akron's Ray C. Bliss Institute of Applied Politics. In 1990, they surveyed 475 evangelical leaders. At that time, 75 percent believed that to change the world they had to change one heart at a time. In the 2000 follow-up survey, 75 percent of 475 leaders had come to the conclusion that the world was changed in two ways: changing individual hearts *and* addressing the systemic and structural evils that exist in all areas of society. This ten-year shift was not happenstance. The NAE invested years of biblical teaching and mentoring to help its constituency recognize the presence and importance of systems in daily life.[34]

In 2001 the NAE realized they lacked a "public theology" to guide the movement.[35] They realized that the issues facing the world and the nation in the twenty-first century would require them to engage in the public square, but realized they were unprepared. Thus, they commenced a three-year process in 2001 that resulted in the 2004 document entitled "For the Health of the Nation: An Evangelical Call to Civic Responsibility." These principles of Christian political engagement included:

1. We work to protect religious freedom and liberty of conscience.
2. We work to nurture family life and protect children.
3. We work to protect the sanctity of human life and to safeguard its nature.
4. We seek justice and compassion for the poor and vulnerable.
5. We work to protect human rights.
6. We seek peace and work to restrain violence.
7. We labor to protect God's creation.[36]

Cizik's work in the NAE Governmental Affairs office has been a major force guiding the evangelical worldview shift since 1990. The NAE board's refusal to dismiss him signals that centrist evangelicals are moving definitively from old Neoplatonic (as Cizik puts it) ways of viewing the world and our relationship to it, to an integrated worldview shaped in large part by the partnership of kingdom and shalom theologies.

As the leading evangelical association in America that embraces an expanded view of the good news, it is making an impact on key issues. Cizik has developed a new Web site to equip evangelicals with the principles of engagement listed above. Focused mainly on creation care, Revision.org offers opportunities to share stories, download information, and stay up-to-date on the issues.

THE TWENTY-FIRST-CENTURY PARACHURCH PREDICAMENT

As he looks around the evangelical world today, Andy Crouch, an editor at *Christianity Today*, does not see parachurch organizations leading in the same way they did in the twentieth century. Crouch predicted that, instead, local megachurches would be the major influencing force of the twenty-first century. I agree with Crouch's assessment that megachurches are reaching twenty thousand each Sunday, while parachurch organizations lack the capacity to reach those numbers. Pastors like Rick Warren, Joel Hunter, T.D. Jakes, Richard Nathan, Floyd Flake, and Bill Hybels inspire members to engage public issues on behalf of justice and, in doing so, they have garnered the respect of an activist generation that is looking for a gospel relevant to their lives and society.[37]

Parachurch organizations have typically been defined as groups that were created alongside churches. Parachurch ministries sprang up throughout the twentieth century with a near-exclusive focus on fulfilling the Great Commission, "Go and make disciples of all nations" (Matthew 28). These parachurch organizations included ministries like the Billy Graham crusades, Young Life youth ministries, InterVarsity, Campus Crusade and the Navigators collegiate ministries, and nondenominational overseas ministries like OMF International. I contend parachurch ministries are not completely out of the picture. Rather, a new generation of collaborators is emerging alongside the church to aid its quest to fulfill the Great Commandment, "You shall love the Lord your God with all your heart, and with all your soul, and with all your mind, and with all your strength. . . . You shall love your neighbor as yourself" (Mark 12:30–31). These collaborators are best described as faith-based advocacy movements, and a groundswell of these movements is rising to the challenges that require the church to engage public issues. Groups like Sojourners, the NAE, the Christian Community Development Association, International Justice Mission (IJM), World Vision, Bread for the World, the Boston Faith and Justice Movement, and the Let Justice Roll Living Wage Campaign are partnering with churches in new ways. In many respects, they are even serving as conduits for unity as a diverse array of denominations adds its voice to the cries of these movements.

Analyzing whether churches or parachurches will lead in the twenty-first century is less important than the message and kind of engagement that will lead evangelical America into the next one hundred years. Evidence says voices crying out for shalom will capture the imaginations of the next generations. A savvy generation, unsatisfied with limited transformation, wants its gospel to be authentic and relevant.

If there is truth in Crouch's assessment of parachurch organizations, it is this: parachurch organizations will be increasingly relevant over the next decade as they exercise the Great Commandment and train their members to exercise not only their citizenship in the kingdom of God but also their citizenship in the world. For example, InterVarsity, a nonprofit organization, cannot lobby legislators about particular pieces of legislation, cannot endorse candidates, and cannot participate in partisan politics. Yet these limitations need not stop its staff from teaching members what it means to engage every aspect of the public life as faith-filled citizens. Thus, they can prepare their students to engage with social movements that address public policies that crush the image of God in others upon graduation.

Greater Los Angeles InterVarsity staff workers Abner Ramos and Scott McLane, who work primarily with African American and Latino students, shared in recent interviews that their work among students of color is challenging their previous notions of mission. Their students struggle under the weight of unjust systems. As a result, Ramos and McLane no longer believe they can carry out the Great Commission without also engaging the Great Commandment.[38]

As the world faces the next century, issues of ethnic and religious conflict, war, global and domestic poverty, the violation of human rights in the United States and abroad all present complex problems beyond the reach of any one sector of society. Missions and Christian community development alone cannot effectively solve the problems. The business sector alone cannot solve the problems. Politics alone cannot solve the problems. Reform necessitates the simultaneous engagement of at least three sectors: the church, the government, and the business sector.

Until recently, prophetic evangelical Christian leadership was largely absent from the public square. Yet this is the realm where shalom-minded evangelical Christians are beginning to make a significant impact. Evangelicals are finding their ultimate choice is not between Republicans or Democrats. Rather, followers of Jesus must engage with social movements that cut across political, religious, and ethnic lines to speak with one voice in support of policies that create justice for all, restore peace to the earth, and bless creation. Oppressive policies crush the image of God on earth. Just policies bless God's image in millions at a time. Blessing or cursing; that is our choice.

Epilogue

On June 28, 2006, I sat a few rows from the front as Barack Obama mounted the stage at the National City Christian Church in Washington, DC. Sitting in the audience with me that day were Christine Lee, Peter Heltzel, and Katie Arner. We were from uptown Manhattan, but we did not meet there. We met each other the previous day on Capitol Hill when Sojourners/Call to Renewal sent us to talk to our congressional representative, Rep. Charles Rangel (D-NY), about the Covenant to Build a New America. Rangel was in session at the time, so we sat down with his general counsel, Jon Sheiner. We were told to expect a fifteen-minute appointment. Soon after we sat down, Sheiner asked us why we were doing this. Why did we care enough to come from New York City to talk with him about raising the minimum wage, cutting the child poverty rate in half in the next ten years, and abiding by the Millennium Development Goals?

I answered, "Because of Matthew 25."

His eyes lit up and he said, "Rangel quotes that to his staff all the time! He says that's why he does what he does! What do you think of that passage?"

I explained, "In Matthew 25, Jesus identifies with the poor. He says, 'What you do or don't do to the least of these, you do or don't do to me.' So, if Jesus identifies with the poor, the marginalized, and the vulnerable, and we are followers of Jesus, then we must identify with the poor, the marginalized, and the vulnerable too. We're here today to let you know how your policies are affecting your constituency in uptown Manhattan." We were with Sheiner for an hour.

Later that day, Heltzel remarked, "We should keep doing this back home in New York." The four of us looked at each other as if to say, Of course. Lee sent the first e-mail a few days after we got home. Soon, we gathered in her living room and asked each other, "What might God have us do? Who might he be calling us to become?" Rachel Anderson came down from Boston to share the story of how the Boston Faith and Justice Network got started. There seemed to be a similar hunger just under the surface in New York City. The church in New York has a long history of engagement with issues of justice. The 1857 Fulton Street Revival that swept the country and helped ignite the abolitionist movement started in New York City. However, the twentieth-century church split also had its origins here. Rauschenbusch reflected on his impoverished neighbors in the city's Hell's Kitchen neighborhood and called the church to reorient the gospel around the social needs of the poor. The fundamentalists reacted, calling the church to a "back to the basics" personal approach to Christian faith.

When we surveyed the condition of the church in New York City in 2006, we found that divide as deep as ever. Yet pastors and Christian leaders on both sides of the split communicated great yearning to come together. What's more, an array of evangelicals, who had largely disengaged from issues of poverty in the political arena, expressed desire to join progressives in their adjuvant advocacy efforts. Could God be calling us to help empower the church in New York City to follow Jesus into the kind of unity that could truly challenge the poverty on our city streets? We met each month, a few more people each time. After six months, we had twelve people and a mission statement: following Christ, uniting the church, ending poverty in New York through spiritual formation, education, and direct advocacy.

Our first action was in response to the fatal police shootings of Sean Bell and Timur Person. Derrick Boykin— northeast organizer for Bread for the World, minister at Walker Memorial Baptist Church, and core member of NY Faith & Justice—led the team that held a public forum on violence in the South Bronx, which a hundred people attended. Katie Arner and InterVarsity staff worker Anna Lee led a simultaneous prayer vigil against violence on the Upper West Side, which another hundred people attended. We had no idea what would come of our work, but a year later a movement to unite the church to fight poverty has taken off in New York City. We called the movement NY Faith & Justice, which has a core group of forty people, partnerships with multiple churches, seminaries, faith organizations, and community-based advocacy groups, and more than three hundred people who participate in NY Faith & Justice events and initiatives. We are ethnically and liturgically diverse; and we are Republican, Democrat, and independent.

If we have learned anything over the past year and a half, it is this: there is a hunger in the church for unity that brings justice and justice that brings unity. Thus, it is incumbent on people who call themselves shalom-minded Jesus followers not to abdicate their responsibility for political engagement in public life. Unaligned evangelicals have tended to avoid politics for fear of the effects of alignment with one party or the other—and rightfully so. Unquestioning alignment to a political party is idolatry. It undermines faith in God. NY Faith & Justice calls believers to align with Jesus, and Jesus aligns himself with the poor. We would say that those who choose to be Republicans should be prophetic Republicans who support public policies and structures that bless the poor. Those who choose to be Democrats should be prophetic Democrats who leverage government, business, and faith communities to bless the poor, so that one day, we might eliminate poverty.

Evangelicals must be true to our faith and our heritage. We must engage public policy in partnership with the oppressed, the marginalized, and the vulnerable. We must partner with individuals whose spirits are crushed every time they hear of another child in the neighborhood lost to violence or drugs. We must give support to the mother who chooses each day whether she will feed her children or pay for her daughter's asthma medication, because they live in a highly polluted neighborhood pushed to the margins of society. Evangelicals must collaborate with the young people in public school systems that fail to provide books or adequately pay qualified teachers to teach bright minds pressed by poverty. Finally, evangelicals must engage for the sake of meeting Jesus face to face in the oppressed, the marginalized, and the vulnerable. In them we see the one who said, "Truly I tell you, just as you did it to the least of these, who are members of my family, you did it to me" (Matthew 25:40). When we do all these things, we will find ourselves walking hand in hand with Jesus, crossing the threshold into freedom land.

Acknowledgments

When I was first asked to consider writing this book, I took the idea to two major communities in my life. First, I went to my NY Faith & Justice (NYFJ) community. The core group gathered in my living room one Sunday night. After I explained the idea for the book, they heaped on blessing through prayers and charges. "Tell the truth," they charged, "and tell it well." Within that community, I owe a special debt of thanks to Peter Heltzel, whose theological scholarship and prophetic vision has built uncommon bridges for the church in New York City. Peter recommended me to The New Press and continues to serve as a faithful advocate and key partner within the movement. The entire NYFJ community has contributed to this project in one way or another; their activism, fueled by love for God and neighbor, has inspired every chapter of this book. I'm particularly indebted to a few who sacrificed priceless time to read early drafts (I stress *early*): they offered feedback, assistance, and prayers at critical times. Their hands, hearts, and eyes made it possible for this book to be completed so quickly. Thank you, Katie Arner, Maritza Crespo, Flavia De Souza, Jose Dobles, Christine Garde, Tina Huang, Mary Hui, Anna Lee, Ashanti Lee, Christine Lee, Jean Schneider, Susan Sharkey, Joanna Yip, and James Winans.

After receiving NYFJ's blessing, I told my family. Later that night, standing in my sister Renee's apartment in Lower Manhattan, blocks from the sight of the 1857 Fulton Street Revival, my mother raised a glass to toast the closing of a circle in my life. Years ago, she perceived my evangelical faith taking me away from the family, and she came to resent that faith. Now, it had led me to ask questions about her activist days with the Student Nonviolent Coordinating Committee: questions about organizing, questions about the role of the church in advocacy, questions about her faith. After clinking glasses, Mom broke into a spontaneous role-play. She morphed instantly into CNN anchor and special correspondent Soledad O'Brien and peppered me with tough questions about the book's point and purpose. When she had seen enough, she said, "Pretty good." Then we cracked up! The process of writing this book has brought us even closer, and my entire family has blessed my time in the writer's cave with mountains of grace and understanding. Thanks to Mom, Dad, and Merry; Hollie, Keith, and Luna; Keith, Lucille, and Nicholas; Renee, Andy, and Alannah; and Ernie, Lisa, Tina, Mar, Ernie, and Elise. Thanks also to Yolanda, Beverly Najuma, Dennis, Cathy, and the Weeks family. I am grateful beyond words for their love and support.

Several other communities and individuals have made priceless contributions to this project. For all that is accurate and valuable about this book, I thank them. They sharpened, deepened, and challenged my understanding of shalom, redemption, restoration, the kingship of God, the kinship of humanity, the substance of justice, and the essence of peace. The limitations of this book are mine.

I am deeply indebted to the sixty-seven evangelical leaders who offered the gift of their time to share their thoughts and feelings about the current state of evangelicalism in the United States. This book could not have been written without their trust, generosity, and insightful points of view. Thank you, Randall Balmer, Ron Benefiel, Kevin Blue, Phil Bowling-Dyer, Tony Campolo, Jeff Carr, Iva Carruthers, Noel Castellanos, Steve Chavis, Richard Cizik, Shane Claiborne, Christian T. Collins Winn, Orlando Crespo, Andy Crouch, Kenya De Alamapo, Jeremy Del Rio, Curtiss Paul DeYoung, Carl Ellis, Michael Emerson, Gordon England, Jeff Farmer, Tom Fortson, Nicole Baker Fulton, Ted Gandy, David P. Gushee, Steve Haas, Mimi Haddad, Paula Harris, Steven Hayner, Obery Hendricks, Alec Hill, Greg Jao, Tim Keller, Jennifer Kottler, Richard Land, Jesse Lava, Terry LeBlanc, Kimberly Lewis, Michael Mata, Christa Mazonne, Christina McDade, Jimmy McGee, Scott McLane, Brian McLaren, Erwin Raphael McManus, Brenda Salter McNeil, Peter Ong, John M. Perkins, Mac Pier, Abner Ramos, Kimberly Ross, Gabriel Salguero, Kevin Saunders, William J. Shaw, Yonce Shelton, Ron Sider, Phil Stump, Adam Taylor, Paul Tokunaga, Richard Twiss, Miroslav Volf, Berten A. Waggoner, Jim Wallis, Rick Warren, and Randy White. A huge debt of thanks goes to Nina Delho and Amy Hitotsubashi, who transcribed the interviews for each one of these leaders. To Amy, I owe a particular debt for her impeccable work and her enthusiastic commitment to the project. She often reminded me of just how amazing it was that we were able to compile such a vast and valuable reservoir of evangelical thought at such a critical juncture in U.S. political and theological history.

Ten years with InterVarsity Christian Fellowship laid the foundation for most of the insights in this book. The depth of gratefulness I feel toward God is beyond words. I was placed in a community with absolutely amazing peers and mentors like Doug and Sandy Schaupp, Jen and Jon Huerta Ball, Una and Henry Lucey-Lee, Donna Noonan, Kevin Blue, Tom Allen, John Teter, Tracey Gee, Jenny and Scott Hall, Brad and Fina Arnold, Anne Hong, Ken Zell, Joyce and Mark Yim, Mailin and Nate Young, Erna Hackett, Gia and Erin Hamilton, Midi Mikasa, Chant Griffin, Yasmeen Muqtasid, Stephanie Capell, Angela Sherman, Dina Burwell, and Jerome Mammen. These women and men served as my refining fire, along with generations of students and scores of national staff partners. They offered me transforming love and high standards of excellence in leadership and biblical interpretation.

Profound gratitude also goes to Samuel Barkat and Jimmy McGee for their prophetic leadership of InterVarsity's Pilgrimage for Reconciliation. Samuel's vision became Jimmy's mission as dozens of InterVarsity staff and students embarked on two four-week explorations of shalom and its destruction on U.S. soil and abroad. Abundant thanks to Terry McGonigal, whose brilliant instruction during the pilgrimage laid the foundation for my exploration of shalom theology. And to Randy and Edith Woodley and Bob and Carol Hunter, I am happily indebted. They led us to engage the histories, ever making connections to the present. They filled in Terry's theological foundation with practical understanding of the ways shalom has been broken on U.S. soil. I give thanks to Glandion Carney, who provided spiritual formation coaching for the journey. As our pilgrimage retraced the Cherokee Trail of Tears and the African experience in America, we felt the weight of the tragedy of the Fall. Glandion's instruction provided reinforcements for our souls. A thank you also to Iva Beranek, His Grace Bishop Joanikije of

Budimlje and Niksic, Peter Kuzmic, Fra. Ivo Markovic, Lazar Predrag Markovic, Maglic Nezir, Boris Peterlin, His Grace Bishop Porfirije of Jegar, Jayme Reaves, Pastor Sasa, Jeff Warner, and Miroslav Volf for their practical instruction in shalom breaking and making during the Croatian/Balkan Pilgrimage for Reconciliation of 2004. My time with them changed the course of my life.

The Los Angeles First Church of the Nazarene and Bresee Institute communities showed me how following Christ went beyond political party lines. Love motivated their quest for unaligned justice, and that love laid a key foundation for my current life's work. I am also deeply grateful for Columbia University professors Paul Martin and Diane Vaughan. Paul Martin's mentorship in the power of religion to bring peace is a constant source of hope. Sociologist Vaughan served as the primary reader for my thesis, which analyzed Religious Right media sources. The material on that subject in this book originated with Dr. Vaughan's inspired instruction.

A heartfelt thank you is in order to Glen Kleinknecht and Campus Crusade for Christ's 1989 Summer in the City Project team, which made John Perkins's *With Justice for All* required reading for all students on my first urban project. They promised us that we would leave New York City at the end of that summer seeing the poor, the marginalized, the vulnerable, and the city itself through God's eyes. They did not disappoint us.

I am deeply indebted to Rita Nakashima Brock for taking of a gamble when she presented my proposal to the editorial board of The New Press. I was an unknown African American female writer and, therefore, an unusual choice to write this book. But Rita's visionary leadership saw something most, including myself, would have missed. I thank her for her unfaltering faith in my ability to deliver more than I believed possible for myself. I thank her for her ever-challenging questions, which pressed me to greater clarity and more "hefty" analysis, as she puts it. If this book is engaging, enriching, challenging, or thought provoking, I dare say it is in large part due to Rita's brilliant guidance.

A great debt of thanks is in order for The New Press. Their genuine interest in evangelical faith and its intersection with the political world has been heartening. I thank The New Press for giving me ample space to tell the story as I see it, without editorial agendas or even a hint of censorship.

Finally, for all the readers who took the time to let me share a few thoughts and a few core convictions, I pray you close these pages with greater hope for our world, greater understanding of evangelicals' place within it, and greater faith that freedom land is not an impossible dream.

Notes

INTRODUCTION

1. See Timothy Smith, *Revivalism and Social Reform: American Protestantism on the Eve of the Civil War* (New York: Harper Torchbooks, 1957).
2. The Pew Forum on Religion and Public Life, "Religion and the 2006 Elections," http://pewforum.org/docs/index.php? DocID=174.
3. Scott Keeter, "Will White Evangelicals Desert the GOP?" *Pew Research Center Publications*, May 2, 2006, http://pew research.org/pubs/22/will-white--evangelicals--desert--the-gop.
4. See Michael Emerson and Christian Smith, *Divided by Faith: Evangelical Religion and the Problem of Race in America* (Oxford: Oxford University Press, 2000).
5. Ibid., 76–77.
6. Ibid., 81.
7. Ibid., 107.
8. This statistic is found in Barry A. Kosmin and Egon Mayer, "American Religious Identification Survey: 2001," Graduate Center of the City University of New York, 12.
9. Curtiss Paul DeYoung, Michael O. Emerson, et al., *United by Faith: The Multiracial Congregation as an Answer to the Problem of Race* (New York: Oxford University Press, 2003), 162–80.

10. Shane Claiborne, *The Irresistible Revolution: Living as an Ordinary Radical* (Grand Rapids, MI: Zondervan, 2006), 188.

CHAPTER 1: ROOTS, FRUITS, AND MUTANTS

1. Timothy L. Smith, *Revivalism and Social Reform: American Protestantism on the Eve of Civil War* (New York: Harper Torchbooks, 1957), 60.

2. Mimi Haddad, interview with author, December 20, 2007; David William Bebbington, *Evangelicalism in Modern Britain: A History from the 1730s to the 1980s* (London: Unwin Hyman, 1989), 2–19.

3. Kathleen A. McAdams, "The Black Experience Within the Episcopal Church: A Chronological Study with Recommendations for Growth," Church Divinity School of the Pacific, September 1998, http://andromeda.rutgers.edu/~lcrew/blackexperience.html.

4. Absalom Jones, "A Thanksgiving Sermon," St. Thomas African Episcopal Church, Philadelphia, PA, 1808, http://anglican history.org/usa/ajones/thanksgiving1808.html.

5. Smith, *Revivalism and Social Reform*, 155.

6. "Religion & Ethics—William Wilberforce: Friendship with John Wesley," BBC Religion and Ethics, http://www.bbc.co.uk/religion/religions/christianity/people/williamwilberforce_7.shtml.

7. "Introduction—William Wilberforce," BBC Religion and Ethics, http://www.bbc.co.uk/religion/religions/christianity/people/williamwilberforce_1.shtml.

8. See Harriet Beecher Stowe Center, http://www.harriet beecherstowecenter.org/life/#childhood.

9. See http://afroamhistory.about.com/library/bltruth_age.htm.

10. *The Narrative of Sojourner Truth*, dictated by Sojourner Truth; ed. Oliver Gilbert (1850). http://digital.library.upenn.edu/women/truth/1850/1850-4.html.

11. "131 Christians Everyone Should Know," Christianity Today.com—Christian History & Biography, http://www.christianity today.com/history/special/131christians/sojourner.html.

12. "The Home of the American Civil War—Biographies: Sojourner Truth," http://www.civilwarhome.com/truthbio.htm.

13. Forrest Wood, *Arrogance of Faith* (New York: Knopf, 1991), 274.

14. Susan Curtis, *A Consuming Faith: The Social Gospel and Modern American Culture* (Baltimore, MD: Johns Hopkins University Press, 1991), 75, 133.

15. Walter Rauschenbusch, *Christianity and the Social Crisis* (New York: Macmillan, 1908), 246.

16. See http://www.rauschenbusch.org/rauschenbusch.php.

17. Martin E. Marty and R. Scott Appleby, "The Enclave Culture," *The Fundamentalism Project: Fundamentalisms Comprehended* (Chicago: University of Chicago Press, 1995), 18.

18. Daniel P. Fuller, *The Unity of the Bible: Unfolding God's Plan for Humanity* (Grand Rapids, MI: Zondervan, 1992), 350.

19. Dallas Willard, *The Divine Conspiracy: Rediscovering the Hidden Life of God* (San Francisco: HarperOne, 1998), 36.

20. Emerson and Smith, *Divided by Faith,* 39.

21. James Cone, "Excerpt: The Religious Cancer of Racism," BeliefNet (2007), http://www.beliefnet.com/story/12/story_1236_1.html.

22. Howard Thurman, *Jesus and the Disinherited* (1949; Boston: Beacon Press, 1976), 11.

23. Ibid., 35.

24. Clarence E. Hardy III, "Imagine a World: Howard Thurman, Spiritual Perception and American Calvinism," *Journal of Religion* 81, no. 1 (Jan. 2001): 81–82.

25. Alton B. Pollard, *Mysticism and Social Change: The Social Witness of Howard Thurman* (New York: Peter Lang, 1992), 24.

26. James H. Cone, "Martin Luther King, Jr., Black Theology—Black Church," *Theology Today* 40, no. 4 (January 1984): 409–20.

27. See Gary Dorrien, *The Making of American Liberal Theology,* vol. 1, *Imagining Progressive Religion, 1805–1900* (Louisville: Westminster John Knox Press, 2001); idem, *The Making of American Liberal Theology,* vol. 2, *Idealism, Realism, and Modernity, 1900–1950* (Louisville: Westminster John Knox Press, 2003); idem, *The Making of American Liberal Theology,* vol. 3, *Crisis, Irony, and Postmodernity: 1950–2005* (Louisville: Westminster John Knox Press, 2006).

28. Peter Heltzel, *Lion on the Loose* (New Haven: Yale University Press, forthcoming).

29. For more information on the Congress on Racial Equality (CORE); go to http://www.core-online.org/.

30. David Dennis, eulogy for James Chaney, August 1964, as quoted in Charles Marsh's *God's Long Summer* (Princeton, NJ: Princeton University Press, 1997), 143.

31. Charles Marsh, *The Beloved Community: How Faith Shapes Social Justice, from the Civil Rights Movement to Today* (New York: Basic Books, 2005), 154.

CHAPTER 2: PROPHETS IN A WILDERNESS

1. Andy Crouch, interview with author, September 16, 2007.

2. Charles Marsh, *The Beloved Community* (New York: Basic Books, 2005), 154.

3. Ibid., 167.

4. Ibid., 168–69.

5. John Perkins, *Let Justice Roll Down* (Ventura, CA: Regal Books, 1976), 222.

6. John Perkins, interview with author, July 2, 2007.

7. Perkins, *Let Justice Roll Down*, 200.

8. Emerson and Smith, *Divided by Faith*, 107, 108, 155, 161.

9. Ibid., 132.

10. John Perkins, interview with author, August 21, 2006.

11. Perkins, interview, July 2, 2007.

12. Marsh, *Beloved Community*, 177.

13. Ibid.

14. Ibid.

15. Tom Skinner, http://www.urbana.org/_articles.cfm?Record Id=185.

16. Tom Skinner, http://www.urbana.org/_articles.cfm?Record Id=186.

17. Jim Wallis, interview with author, September 6, 2007.

18. Ibid.

19. Tony Campolo, interview with author, June 20, 2007.

20. Ron Sider, interview with author, June 5, 2007.

21. Ibid.

22. Ron Sider, *Just Generosity: A New Vision for Overcoming Poverty in America* (Grand Rapids, MI: Baker Books, 1999), 13.

23. Ibid., 5.

CHAPTER 3: JILTED AND FRAMED

1. Randall Balmer, *Thy Kingdom Come: An Evangelical's Lament* (New York: Basic Books, 2006), ix.

2. See http://www.irs.ustreas.gov/pub/irs-tege/eotopicd8o.pdf.

3. See http://caselaw.lp.findlaw.com/cgi-bin/getcase.pl?court=US&vol=461&invol=574.

4. Ibid.

5. Ibid.

6. Balmer, *Thy Kingdom Come*, 13.

7. Ibid., 14. The content of the November 1990 Ethics and Public Policy Center Conference is also meticulously documented in Michael Cromartie's *No Longer Exiles* (Washington, DC: Ethics and Public Policy Center, 1993), 26, a collection of four papers, followed by commentary, originally presented at the conference.

8. Ibid., 15.

9. Ibid.

10. See http://www.bju.edu/about/history/gville3.html.

11. The material discussed in this section has been adapted from my master's thesis, *The Religious Right: Collective Action through Twisted Justice* (Columbia University, 2006).

12. William A Gamson, *Talking Politics* (Cambridge: Cambridge University Press, 1992), 3.

13. Ibid.

14. Ibid., 84–85, 178.

15. William J. Stuntz, "Sad but Noble," *Citizen*, March 2006, 18.

16. Ibid., 23.

17. Ibid.

18. John Fitzpatrick (*World* circulation manager), e-mail correspondence, July 25, 2006.

19. Marvin Olasky, "Nuke Nightmare," *World* February 25, 2006, http://www.worldmag.com/articles/11552.

20. Ibid.

21. Ibid.

22. Peggy Noonan, "What I Saw at the Devastation," *Wall Street Journal*, September 13, 2001, http://www.opinionjournal.com/columnists/pnoonan/?id=95001113.

23. Olasky, http://www.worldmag.com/articles/11552.

24. Balmer, *Thy Kingdom Come*, 12.

25. Guttmacher Institute, "Trends in Abortion in the United States, 1973–2005," January 2008, http://www.guttmacher.org/presentations/trends.pdf.

26. *Parents Involved in Community Schools v. Seattle School District No. 1 Et Al.*, 551 U.S. (2007), 28, http://www.supremecourtus.gov/opinions/06pdf/05-908.pdf.

CHAPTER FOUR: BROKEN PROMISES?

1. See http://www.promisekeepers.org/about/pkhistory.

2. Interview with author, December 14, 2007.

3. Bill McCartney, *From Ashes to Glory* (Nashville, TN: Thomas Nelson, 1995), 292.

4. Michael Emerson and Christian Smith, *Divided by Faith: Evangelical Religion and the Problem of Race in America* (Oxford: Oxford University Press, 2000), 65.

5. Ibid., 68.

6. McCartney as quoted in ibid., 67.

7. Michael Emerson, interview with author, December 18, 2007.

8. Tom Fortson, Gordon England, and Steve Charis, interview with the author, December 14, 2007.

9. Ibid.

10. Emerson, interview.

11. Noel Castellanos, interview with author, December 18, 2007.

12. Ibid.

13. Emerson, interview.

14. John Perkins, interview with author, August 21, 2007.

15. Emerson, interview.

16. Ibid.

17. Brenda Salter McNeil, interview with author, December 21, 2007.

18. David Murrow, *Why Men Hate Going to Church* (Nashville, TN: Thomas Nelson, 2005), 4.

19. There are three theological views of proper relationship between the genders. The first is the traditionalist view, which holds a patriarchal view of gender roles. The second is the complementarian view, which espouses that differing, nonoverlapping roles are reserved for men and women in marriage, church leadership, and in the marketplace. Third, the egalitarian view maintains that there are no biblically prescribed roles for men and women in any sphere of life. The PK movement ascribes to the complementarian view.

20. Bryan W. Brickner, *The Promise Keepers: Politics and Promises* (Lanham, MD: Lexington Books, 1999), 79.

21. Ibid.

22. See http://www.promisekeepers.org/about/statementoffaith.

23. Fortson, England, and Chavis, interview.

24. Jackie Loh, e-mail correspondence, December 23, 2007.

25. Many of the prime opponents of the ERA were evangelical Christians. This is highly ironic since it was Christians who planted the seeds of the women's suffrage movement in the early nineteenth century.

26. Emerson, interview.

27. Emerson and Smith, *Divided by Faith*, 78.

28. National Association of Evangelicals Web site, http://www.nae.net/index.cfm?FUSEACTION=editor.page&pageID=211&IDCategory=9.

29. Fortson, England, and Chavis, interview.

CHAPTER FIVE: APOLOGIES AND POWER POLITICS

1. The Southern Baptist Convention, "Resolution on Racial Reconciliation on the 150th Anniversary of the Southern Bap-

tist Convention," June 1995, http://www.sbc.net/resolutions/am Resolution.asp?ID=899 (written by Richard Land for the Convention).

2. Ibid.

3. W. Andrew Tillman and William M. Tillman Jr., "The Rise, Decline, and Fall of Christian Life Commission Entities and Voices," *High Beam Encyclopedia: Baptist History and Heritage*, http://www.encyclopedia.com/doc/1G1-155475835.html.

4. Charles Marsh, *God's Long Summer* (Princeton, NJ: Princeton University Press, 1997), 98.

5. Ibid., 101.

6. Ibid., 114–15.

7. Richard Land, interview with author, November 16, 2007.

8. Ibid.

9. Ibid.

10. Ibid.

11. Ibid.

12. Ibid.

13. Ibid.

14. Ibid.

15. Ibid.

16. Southern Baptist Convention, "Resolution."

17. Land, interview.

18. Southern Baptist Convention, "Resolution."

19. Land, interview.

20. Ibid.

21. Southern Baptist Convention, "Resolution."

22. Ibid.

23. Land, interview.

24. Gustav Neibuhr, "Baptist Group Votes to Repent Stand on Slaves," *New York Times*, June 21, 1995, http://query.nytimes.com/gst/fullpage.html?res=990CE4DA163BF932A15755Co A963958260&sec=&spon=&pagewanted=all.

25. Land, interview.

26. Neibuhr, "Baptist Group Votes."

27. Ibid.

28. Ibid.

29. Southern Baptist Convention, "Resolution."

30. Land, interview.

31. Anonymous, interview with author, 2007.

32. Land, interview.

33. Urban Institute, "Welfare Reform Roundtable: Reviewing a Decade, Previewing the Future," July 25, 2006, http://www.urban.org/Pressroom/events/welfarereform.cfm.

34. National Baptist Convention, "The People Have Spoken," January–February 2007, http://www.nationalbaptist.com/Index.cfm?FuseAction=Page&PageID=1000384.

35. The first two of these responses (a woman's right to choose and same-sex marriage) are, obviously, personal issues that carry moral weight for people on both sides of the debate. The third (the creationist/evolutionist debate) may not seem a personal or moral issue; however, for the staunch creationist, evolution is not simply a matter of science or education. It is an affirmation of personal faith, which guides the moral compass. The polemicized position goes like this: If God did not create the universe, then human beings are simply matter with no ultimate purpose and no inherent worth. If that is so, then we have no mandate toward any particular moral standard. (See chapter 7 for continued discussion of this debate.) Thus, the creationism v. evolutionism debate is or is not a personal or moral debate, depending on whether or not one believes in a Creator God.

36. William J. Shaw, "Position Statements," National Baptist Convention, USA, July 2004, http://www.nationalbaptist.com/images/documents/91.pdf.

37. William J. Shaw, interview with author, January 9, 2008.

38. Emerson, interview.

39. Emerson and Smith, *Divided by Faith*, 136, 155.

40. *The Baptist Faith and Message* (2000), http://www.sbc.net/bfm/bfm2000.asp#vi.

41. William E. Hull, "Women and the Southern Baptist Convention," *Christian Ethics Today*, issue 29, vol. 6, no. 4, http://www.christianethicstoday.com/Issue/029/Women%20and%20the%20Southern%20Baptist%20Convention%20By%20William%20E%20Hulle_029_10_.htm#_edn5.

42. Ibid.

43. Ibid.

44. "The Baptist Faith and Message," http://www.sbc.net/bfm/.

CHAPTER SIX: THE RECONCILIATION GENERATION

1. David W. Bebbington, "Martyrs for the Truth: Fundamentalists in Britain," in Diana Wood, ed., *Martyrs and Martyrologies*, Studies in Church History, vol. 30 (Oxford: Blackwell Publishers, 1993), 421.

2. Steven Hayner, interview with author, December 17, 2001.

3. Pete Hammond and Neil Rendall, "InterVarsity's Journey Toward Multiethnicity," 2006, http://www.intervarsity.org/mem/page.php?id=1252.

4. Hayner, interview.

5. Ibid.

6. Ibid.

7. Hammond and Rendall, "InterVarsity's Journey"

8. Ibid.

9. Hayner, interview.

10. Ibid.

11. Mimi Haddad, interview with author, December 20, 2007.

12. See http://www.intervarsity.org/mem/page.php?id=1252.

13. Ron Benefiel, interview with author, December 14, 2007.

14. Paula Harris, e-mail correspondence, December 30, 2007.

15. Paula Harris, interview with author, December 30, 2007.

16. Evan Adams, "Youth and Tradition," Urbana 1967 Convention, http://www.urbana.org/_articles.cfm?RecordId=1068.

17. Carl Ellis, interview with author, December 24, 2007.

18. Hammond and Rendall, "InterVarsity's Journey."

19. Ibid.

20. Hayner, interview.

21. Harris, interview.

22. Brenda Salter McNeil, "Calling Forth a Reconciliation Generation," Urbana 2000 Missions Convention, http://www.urbana.org/u2000.dec28p.brendasm.cfm.

23. Ibid.

24. Brenda Salter McNeil, *A Credible Witness: Reflections on Power, Evangelism and Race* (Chicago, IL: InterVarsity Press, 2008), 75.

25. Hayner, interview.

26. Harris, interview.

27. See http://www.rapidnet.com/~jbeard/bdm/Psychology/ivcf/urbana90.htm.

28. Hayner, interview.

29. Ray Aldred, "Cross-Cultural Conversion," Urbana 2003 Missions Convention, http://www.urbana.org/u2003.text.item.cfm?TextItemId=94.

30. Scott McLane, interview with author, December 26, 2007.

31. Ibid.

32. Alec Hill, interview with author, June 4, 2007.

33. Ibid.

34. Randy White, interview with author, June 14, 2007.

35. Orlando Crespo, interview with author, May 31, 2007.

36. Phil Stump, interview with author, December 11, 2007.

37. *The Four Spiritual Laws* was a little gold booklet that served as Campus Crusade's main evangelistic tool from the mid-1960s through the mid-1990s. The Four Laws communicated the gospel message in terms of spiritual laws that mirror the physical laws of the universe. Law one, God loves you and offers a wonderful plan for your life. Law two, man is sinful and separated from God. Therefore, he cannot know and experience God's love and plan for his life. Law three, Jesus Christ is God's only provision for man's sin. Through Him you can know and experience God's love and plan for your life. Law four, we must individually receive Jesus Christ as Savior and Lord; then we can know and experience God's love and plan for our lives.

38. Ted Gandy, interview with author, September 11, 2007.

39. Willard, *The Divine Conspiracy*, 36–37.

40. The Great Commission is found in Matthew 28:18 when Jesus says to his disciples, "All authority in heaven and on earth has been given to me. Go therefore and make disciples of all nations, baptizing them in the name of the Father and of the Son and of the

Holy Spirit, and teaching them to obey everything that I have commanded you. And remember, I am with you always, to the end of the age." The Great Commandment is found in Luke 10.

    41. Gandy, interview.

CHAPTER SEVEN: GOOD NEWS . . . AGAIN!

    1. Rick Warren, interview with author, January 29, 2008.

    2. Iva E. Carruthers, interview with author, June 28, 2007.

    3. Iva E. Carruthers, Fredrick D. Haynes Jr., and Jeremiah A. Wright, ed., *Blow the Trumpet in Zion: Global Vision and Action for the 21st-century Black Church* (Minneapolis: Fortress Press, 2005), 18.

    4. Wikipedia, "Perfection," http://en.wikipedia.org/wiki/Perfection.

    5. Miroslav Volf, *Free of Charge: Giving and Forgiving in a Culture Stripped of Grace* (Grand Rapids, MI: Zondervan, 2005), 38.

    6. Steve Haas, interview with author, January 11, 2008.

    7. Jeff Zolitor, "Judaism, the Jewish Jesus and the Politics of Judea," Congress of Secular Jewish Organizations, http://csjo.org/pages/essays/essayjewthe manjesus.htm.

    8. Obery Hendricks, interview with author, December 28, 2008.

    9. The problem with the creationist/evolutionist debate is that it is cast in an either/or framework. Either one is creationist or she is an evolutionist. The two ideas tend to stand at an unnecessary impasse. Many people believe in the concept of intelligent design *and* believe in some variation on the theory of evolution. Thus, it is possible, even more biblically accurate, I assert, for students of the Bible to acknowledge a Creator of an ordered world. However, they must also acknowledge that the Creator gave humans no scientific document to help us understand exactly "how" the world was created. In this both/and theology, the Creator gave Genesis 1 and 2 as texts written in the form of poetry and story to communicate truths about God, humanity, and our relationships with each other and the rest of creation, not as a scientific document. The fact

that Genesis offers no scientific explanation is made obvious as one compares the orders of creation presented in the two accounts. They are different. For example, in the Genesis 1 account, God made animals and vegetation before humans. In the Genesis 2 account, God made humans first.

In addition, creationists who stand in the tradition of the Scopes trial make the mistake of reinforcing a polemic that demands their particular interpretation of scripture be taught as standard Christian belief in public schools. This is troublesome because there is no standard Christian belief. There are variations on a theme—God the Creator created the world. After that, there is debate even within Christendom as to the question of *how*. Therefore to mandate a particular Christian worldview be taught as the standard is dishonest and unfair. Further, it places public school teachers in the inappropriate position of having to teach something they don't necessarily understand or believe.

10. All translations derived using James H. Strong, *Strong's Exhaustive Concordance* (Grand Rapids, MI: Baker Books, 1992).

11. Volf, *Free of Charge*, 27.

12. Walter Brueggemann, *Peace* (St. Louis, MO: Chalice Press, 2001), 2–4.

CHAPTER EIGHT: ENGAGE

1. James Farmer, interview with author, January 9, 2008.

2. Jim Wallis, interview with author, June 28, 2006.

3. Barack Obama, "The Audacity of Hope," 2004 Democratic National Convention Keynote Address, July 27, 2004, http://www.americanrhetoric.com/speeches/convention2004/barackobama2004dnc.htm.

4. Jeff Carr, interview with author, June 28, 2006.

5. Jack Shafer, "The Rebellion of the Talking Heads," *Slate.com*, September 2, 2005, http://www.slate.com/id/2125581/.

6. Carr, interview.

7. Barack Obama, "Call to Renewal Keynote Address," Washington, DC, June 28, 2006.

8. Ibid.

9. Ibid.

10. Ibid.

11. Ibid.

12. Kenya De Alamapo, interview with author, June 27, 2007.

13. Ibid.

14. Ibid.

15. Kevin Saunders, interview with author, June 27, 2007.

16. Jesse Lava, interview with author, July 19, 2007.

17. Jesse Lava, interview with author, June 27, 2006.

18. Lava, interview, July 19, 2007.

19. Ibid.

20. Ibid.

21. David P. Gushee, interview with author, June 20, 2007.

22. Ibid.

23. Ibid.

24. Ibid.

25. Rachel Anderson, interview with author, January 6, 2008.

26. Ibid.

27. Jennifer Kottler, interview with author, July 22, 2007.

28. Ibid.

29. "Our Mission," Let Justice Roll Living Wage Campaign Web site, http://www.letjusticeroll.org/mission.html.

30. Richard Cizik, interview with author, July 10, 2007.

31. Ibid.

32. Ibid.

33. Ibid.

34. Ibid.

35. Ibid.

36. Richard Cizik, "The United Nations' MDG Campaign for a Better World" (speech, On the Role of American Religious Communities in Achieving the Millennium Development Goals: A Consultation, June 8, 2005), http://www.globalinterfaithed.org/cizik.htm.

37. Andy Crouch, interview with author, September 16, 2007.

38. Abner Ramos, interview with author, December 24, 2007; Scott McLane, interview with author, December 27, 2007.